AMERICA'S
TEST KITCHEN

THE
COMPLETE
BAKING BOOK
FOR YOUNG CHEFS

sourcebooks
eXplore

Published by Sourcebooks eXplore, an imprint of
    Sourcebooks Kids
P.O. Box 4410, Naperville, Illinois 60567-4410
(630) 961-3900
sourcebookskids.com

This product conforms to all applicable CPSC and CPSIA standards.

Source of Production: Worzalla, Stevens Point,
    Wisconsin, USA
Date of Production: June 2021
Run Number: 5021917

Printed and bound in the United States of America.
WOZ 19 18 17 16 15 14 13 12 11 10 9

AMERICA'S TEST KITCHEN

Editor in Chief: Molly Birnbaum
Executive Food Editor: Suzannah McFerran
Senior Editors: Katie Leaird, Sarah Wilson
Associate Editors: Afton Cyrus, Sasha Marx
Test Cook: Katie Callahan
Deputy Editor, Education: Kristin Sargianis
Photography Director: Julie Bozzo Cote
Art Director: Emma Kurman-Faber
Senior Staff Photographer: Daniel J. van Ackere
Staff Photographers: Steve Klise, Kevin White
Food Styling: Elle Simone, Ashley Moore, Kendra Smith,
    Sally Staub
Photography Producer: Meredith Mulcahy
Photoshoot Kitchen Team:
    Manager: Tim McQuinn
    Lead Test Cook: Jessica Rudolph
    Assistant Test Cooks: Eric Haessler, Sarah Ewald,
    Jacqueline Gochenouer, Hannah Fenton
Imaging Manager: Lauren Robbins
Production and Imaging Specialists: Dennis Noble,
    Jessica Voas, Amanda Yong
Senior Manager, Publishing Operations: Taylor Argenzio
Senior Copy Editor: Jillian Campbell

Chief Creative Officer: Jack Bishop
Executive Editorial Directors: Julia Collin Davison,
    Bridget Lancaster

CONTENTS

TREATS TASTE BETTER WHEN YOU MAKE THEM YOURSELF

One of the best things about baked goods is that it's almost impossible not to share them with family and friends. And when these treats are shared, they make people feel happy. So by baking, you're essentially just making the people you love feel good. Plus, baked goods taste better when you make them yourself!

Like our first cookbook for kids, *The Complete Cookbook for Young Chefs*, this book is kid-tested and kid-approved. That means there are thousands of other kids just like you out there, making these recipes and sharing them with their friends and family, loving the process and the results. When making this book, we had more than 4,000 kids testing each and every recipe, sending us feedback (and even coming into our office to cook in the test kitchen), and letting us know what worked well and what could use improvement. You'll see a handful of these recipe testers in the pages of this book. Thank you to everyone who helped make this book as delicious as possible!

Baking is a science as well as an art, so as you begin baking on your own, don't be surprised if you have questions (never hesitate to ask an adult) and you make some mistakes (we've all been there). Mistakes are an important part of the baking and cooking process. Luckily, they're often still pretty delicious.

And most important? Have fun with this book. Use it to be creative. And take pride in all that you're about to accomplish.

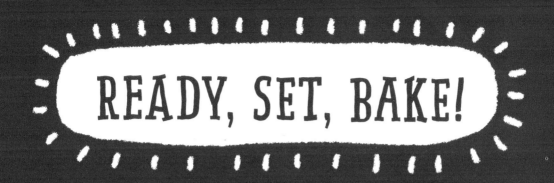

READY, SET, BAKE!

UNDERSTANDING THE SYMBOLS IN THIS BOOK

To help you find the right recipe for you, this book relies on a system of symbols to designate skill level as well as type of cooking required.

1 hat:
beginner
recipe

2 hats:
intermediate
recipe

3 hats:
advanced
recipe

  = requires use of knife

= requires use of microwave

= requires use of stovetop

= requires use of oven

= no knives or heat required

HOW TO USE THE RECIPES IN THIS BOOK

Baking (or cooking) from a recipe is actually a three-step process, and the recipes in this book are written to reflect that, with three distinct sections. The key to successful (and easy) baking is, in our humble opinion, all about organization. If you prepare all your ingredients (do the measuring or melting) and gather all your equipment before you start baking, then you won't have to run around the kitchen looking for that last pan or realize that you're out of flour.

PREPARE INGREDIENTS: Start with the list of ingredients and prepare them as directed. Measure ingredients, melt butter, and chop as needed. Wash fruits and vegetables. You can use small prep bowls to keep ingredients organized.

GATHER BAKING EQUIPMENT: Once all your ingredients are ready, put all the tools you will need to follow the recipe instructions on the counter.

START BAKING!: It's finally time to mix ingredients together and bake them in the oven. Any ingredients that need to be prepped at the last minute will have instruction within the recipe itself.

4 SECRETS TO SUCCESS IN BAKING

SECRET #1: READ CAREFULLY

If you're learning to bake, you're probably reading a recipe. It will take some time to understand the language used in baking recipes (see Decoding Bakingspeak, page 8).

• Start with the key stats. How much food does the recipe make? How long will it take? (Some bread recipes can take time over the course of two whole days.) When you're hungry for breakfast or an after-noon snack, choose a recipe that takes less than an hour.

• Make sure you have the right ingredi-ents and equipment. Make sure you have the right cake pan before you start mixing your cake batter. Make sure you have yeast before you start making your bread dough.

• It's important to follow the recipe for most things in this book. (Baking is precise, and the ratios of ingredients are important!) But, as in our first book, we have "Make It Your Way" sidebars throughout the book to help inspire you to get creative wherever you can, custom-izing recipes to your taste.

SECRET #2: STAY FOCUSED

Baking requires a lot of attention—every single ingredient is important to the success of the recipe.

• Measure VERY carefully (see page 10 for more tips). Even more than in cooking, the amount of each ingredient in a baking recipe can make a difference. Too much (or not enough) yeast or baking powder or baking soda can ruin a recipe.

• Recipes are written with both visual ("bake until golden brown") and time cues ("bake for 22 minutes"). Bakers use all their senses—sight, hearing, touch, smell, and taste—in the kitchen.

• Many recipes contain time ranges, such as "bake until golden brown, 22 to 26 minutes." These ranges account for differ-ences in various ovens. Set your timer for the lowest number. If the food isn't done yet (see page 15 for tips on testing for doneness), you can keep on baking it.

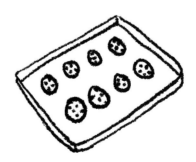

SECRET #3: PRACTICE SAFETY

Ovens can be dangerous (they're hot!). Always ask an adult for help if you're in doubt.

• Use the knife that's right for you. This will depend on the size of your hands and your skill level.

• Hot stovetops and ovens can cause painful burns. Assume that anything on the stovetop (including the pan's handle and lid) is hot. Everything inside the oven is definitely hot. Always use oven mitts.

• Wash your hands before cooking.

• Wash your hands after touching raw eggs.

• Never let foods you eat raw (such as sliced berries) touch foods you will cook (such as raw eggs).

• Don't ever leave something on the stove unattended. Always turn off the stove and oven when you're done.

SECRET #4: MISTAKES ARE MORE THAN OK

Mistakes are a big part of baking and one of the best ways to learn. Don't sweat it. Try to figure out what you would do differently next time. Maybe you should have set a timer so you would remember to check the cookies in the oven. Maybe you should have measured more carefully.

• If your food isn't perfect, don't worry. A misshapen cookie is still delicious. If you enjoy your "mistakes," everyone else will enjoy them too. Remember: You baked! That's so cool.

DECODING BAKINGSPEAK

WHISK: To combine ingredients with a whisk until uniform or evenly incorporated. For example, you whisk together dry ingredients such as flour, sugar, baking powder, and baking soda.

STIR: To combine ingredients in a bowl or cooking vessel, often with a rubber spatula or wooden spoon.

WHIP: To combine vigorously with a whisk or electric mixer, with the goal of adding air to increase the volume of the ingredients (such as whipping cream or egg whites).

BEAT: To combine vigorously with a whisk, fork, or electric mixer, often with the goal of adding air to increase the volume of the ingredients (such as beating butter and sugar together to make cookie dough).

SCRAPE: To push ingredients on the sides of a bowl, pan, blender jar, or food processor back into the center—or out of a bowl into a pan. A rubber spatula is the best tool for this job.

KNEAD: To mix and move dough with your hands (or a stand mixer) in order to develop the gluten structure of the dough.

RISE: When dough rises, yeast creates gas bubbles that cause the dough to expand and develop flavor.

PEEL: To remove the outer skin, rind, or layer from food, usually a piece of fruit or a vegetable. Often done with a vegetable peeler.

ZEST: To remove the flavorful colored outer peel from a lemon, lime, or orange (the colored skin is called the zest). Does not include the bitter white layer (called pith) under the zest.

CHOP: To cut food with a knife into small pieces.
• Chopped fine = ⅛- to ¼-inch pieces
• Chopped = ¼- to ½-inch pieces
• Chopped coarse = ½- to ¾-inch pieces
Use a ruler to understand the different sizes.

MINCE: To cut food with a knife into ⅛-inch pieces or smaller.

WHAT'S UP WITH INGREDIENTS?

FLOUR: Stock all-purpose flour in your pantry—it works well in a wide range of recipes, from cakes to cookies. Sometimes we call for cake flour (which contains less structure-building protein), bread flour (which contains more), or whole-wheat flour.

VEGETABLE OIL SPRAY: We often call for this sprayable oil to coat cake pans and muffin tins and help prevent baked goods from sticking. Sometimes we call for "vegetable oil spray with flour," also known as "baking spray," which is just what it sounds like—sprayable oil with added flour. This helps with particularly sticky batters or batters that need a little help rising in the pan.

EGGS: Our recipes call for large eggs. It's important in baking recipes to use the size the recipe calls for.

BAKING POWDER & BAKING SODA: These leaveners are essential in pancakes, muffins, cakes, cookies, and more. They are not interchangeable.

YEAST: Yeast is a single-celled fungi (yes, it's alive!). It metabolizes sugars and creates carbon dioxide, helping bread rise. Yeast can be fresh or dried. We use dried yeast in this book—either instant or rapid-rise. (See page 78 for more on yeast.)

SUGAR: Granulated white sugar is the most commonly used sweetener, although some recipes call for confectioners' (powdered) sugar or brown sugar (use either light or dark unless the recipe specifies otherwise). When we call for "sugar" in our recipes, we are referring to granulated white sugar.

MILK & DAIRY: Milk, cream, half-and-half (made with half milk and half cream), yogurt, and sour cream are common ingredients. It's important in baking recipes to use the type of dairy called for (don't substitute low-fat milk for cream).

VANILLA EXTRACT: Vanilla is one of the world's most popular flavors. It comes in two forms: pure vanilla extract, which is made from the seed pods of vanilla orchid vines, and synthetic vanilla, which is made in a lab. Either will work in our recipes.

CHOCOLATE: There are many different types of chocolate—bittersweet, semisweet, milk, white. They all have different percentages of cacao (the darkest chocolate contains the most, and white chocolate contains none).

COCOA POWDER (DUTCH): This unsweetened powder is made from grinding the seeds of a cacao tree. In baking, we call for Dutch-processed cocoa powder, which has been processed in a way that raises the cocoa powder's pH, and makes it taste more fully chocolaty and have a darker color. (See page 159 for more on cocoa powder.)

SALT: There are many kinds of salt. Most of the recipes in this book were tested with table salt (the kind with fine crystals that you keep in a shaker). You can use larger, chunkier kosher salt or sea salt, but you may need a bit more of it.

BUTTER: Use unsalted butter. Salted butter is great on toast but can make some foods too salty.

⎯⎯ HOW TO WEIGH AND MEASURE ⎯⎯

It's important to measure accurately when baking. There are two ways to measure ingredients: by weight, using a scale, or by volume, using measuring cups and spoons.

USING A SCALE

Turn on the scale and place the bowl on the scale. Then press the "tare" button to zero out the weight (that means that the weight of the bowl won't be included).

Slowly add your ingredient to the bowl until you reach the desired weight. Here we are weighing 5 ounces of all-purpose flour (which is equal to 1 cup).

HOW TO MEASURE DRY AND LIQUID INGREDIENTS

DRY INGREDIENTS should be measured in dry measuring cups—small metal or plastic cups with handles. Each set has cups of varying sizes. Dip the measuring cup into the ingredient and sweep away the excess with the back of a butter knife.

LIQUID INGREDIENTS should be measured in a liquid measuring cup (a larger clear plastic or glass cup with lines on the side, a big handle, and a pour spout). Set the measuring cup level on the counter and bend down to read the bottom of the concave arc at the liquid's surface. This is known as the meniscus line. Note that small amounts of both dry and liquid ingredients are measured with small measuring spoons.

HOW TO MEASURE ICE WATER

When ice water is called for in a recipe, it is essential that the water is very, very cold—but we do not want the ice to end up in the food! Here is the best way to measure out ice water:

Fill up a large glass with ice and water. Keep this in the refrigerator until right before you need to use it—this is VERY important! Place a fine-mesh strainer over a bowl or liquid measuring cup. Place the bowl or measuring cup on a scale (if using) and tare the scale. Then pour the water through the fine-mesh strainer to measure the desired amount of water. Discard the ice.

MICROWAVE 101

Most microwaves have a power setting that lets you cook things at reduced power levels. It's important to melt butter and chocolate at 50 percent of full power. The controls can vary from microwave to microwave, but often you have to set the power level before setting the time. Ask an adult for help.

Why do we let baked goods cool if they're still delicious when warm?

We know, we know: no one wants to wait for their delicious treats to cool. But it is important in most cases. Breads can deflate, be hard to slice, and taste gummy if they're still hot. And you definitely don't want to try to frost a hot cake, cupcake, or cookie (unless you're looking for frosting soup).

What's the best way to store baked goods?

Have leftovers? It's important to always let your baked goods cool completely before storing for later. Then, place them in airtight containers or zipper-lock plastic bags and keep them on the counter for anywhere from two to four days. Note that baked goods stored in the refrigerator will get stale faster.

Speaking of… Why does bread get stale?

Excellent question. Bread often gets stale, or dry and crusty, after a couple of days thanks to something called retrogradation. When bread is baking, the liquid in the dough hydrates the starch in the flour, causing it to soften and resulting in soft, pliable bread. But when bread sits out after it's been baked, the starches start to crystallize, trapping a lot of that water within that new crystalline structure. There is still liquid there, but it's hiding, making the bread feel all dry and crusty. One way to improve stale bread is by toasting it. The heat releases all that hidden water, reviving your slice of bread.

What is gluten, anyway?

Yes, we talk about gluten all the time. But it's very important in bread (it's not just something people are allergic to). Why? Gluten is a protein. It is created when flour and water mix. The long strands of protein are kind of like elastic bands for your hair, and they have the ability to expand. This is particularly important when bread rises, because the network of gluten proteins can trap air inside the bread dough, helping it grow tall. Kneading or mixing helps the gluten develop into a strong network that can trap lots of air, which helps give bread a nice chewy texture.

Why do you flour the counter sometimes but not all the time when working with dough?

Doughs have different textures, depending on what you're making. Some doughs are very sticky, and in order to shape them into scones or rolls, you need to sprinkle a little flour onto the counter and your hands so the dough doesn't stick to everything. Other doughs are relatively dry, so there's no need to add extra flour. Don't worry, our recipes will tell you when you need to use a little extra flour.

10 ESSENTIAL PREP STEPS

HOW TO MELT BUTTER

Butter can be melted in a small saucepan on the stove (use medium-low heat), but we think the microwave is easier.

1. Cut butter into 1-tablespoon pieces. Place butter in microwave-safe bowl.

2. Place bowl in microwave and cover bowl with small plate. Heat butter at 50 percent power (see page 11) until melted, 30 to 60 seconds (longer if melting a lot of butter). Watch butter and stop microwave as soon as butter has melted. Use oven mitts to remove bowl from microwave.

HOW TO SOFTEN BUTTER

When taken straight from the refrigerator, butter is quite firm. For some baking recipes and many frostings, you need to soften butter before trying to combine it with other ingredients. This is just a fancy term for letting the temperature of butter rise from 35 degrees (its refrigerator temperature) to 65 degrees (cool room temperature). This takes about 1 hour. But here are two ways to speed things up.

Counter Method: Cut butter into 1-inch pieces (to create more surface area). Place butter on plate and wait about 30 minutes. Once butter gives to light pressure (try to push your fingertip into butter), it's ready to use.

Microwave Method: Cut butter into 1-inch pieces and place on microwave-safe plate. Heat in microwave at 50 percent power (see page 11) for 10 seconds. Check butter with fingertip test. Heat for another 5 to 10 seconds if necessary.

HOW TO CRACK AND SEPARATE EGGS

Unless you are hard-cooking eggs, you need to start by cracking them open. In some recipes, you will need to separate the yolk (the yellow part) and white (the clear part) and use them differently. Cold eggs are much easier to separate.

1. To crack: Gently hit side of egg against flat surface of counter or cutting board.

2. Pull shell apart into 2 pieces over bowl. Let yolk and white drop into bowl. Discard shell.

3. To separate yolk and white: Use your hand to very gently transfer yolk to second bowl.

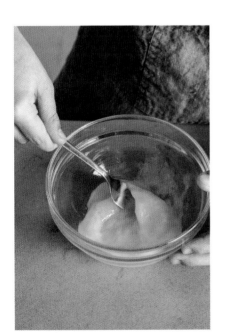

HOW TO CRACK AND LIGHTLY BEAT EGG

Sometimes you need an egg wash (a beaten egg) to brush over dough, which helps with browning and shine or helps seal dough together.

Gently hit side of egg against flat surface of counter or cutting board. Pull shell apart into 2 pieces over bowl. Let yolk and white drop into bowl. Discard shell. Use fork to beat egg until well combined. Hint: moving the fork quickly from side to side works better than moving it in a circle.

Clean

Crumbs attached

HOW TO TEST FOR DONENESS WITH A TOOTHPICK

Here's an easy way to test baked goods (muffins, cupcakes, cakes, brownies, and more) for doneness. See individual recipes—in some cases the toothpick should come out clean, while in other recipes a few crumbs are OK. If you see wet, sticky batter, keep on baking.

Insert toothpick into center of baked good, then remove it. Examine toothpick for crumbs and evaluate it against directions in specific recipe to determine if baked good is ready to come out of oven.

HOW TO MAKE AN ALUMINUM FOIL SLING

Lining a baking pan with two pieces of aluminum foil makes it super easy to get baked brownies, cakes, and even granola bars out of the pan. The pieces of foil should be the same width as the pan and long enough to hang over the sides.

For an 8-inch square pan, both sheets of foil should measure 8 inches across and roughly 13 inches long.

For a 13-by-9-inch pan, one sheet should measure 13 inches wide and the other 9 inches wide. Both sheets should be about 18 inches long.

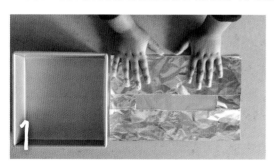

1. Fold 2 long sheets of aluminum foil to match width of baking pan. Sheets should be same width for square pans but different widths for rectangular pans.

2. Lay sheets of foil in pan so that sheets are perpendicular to each other. Let extra foil hang over edges of pan. Push foil into corners and up sides of pan, smoothing foil so it rests against pan.

HOW TO GREASE A BAKING PAN OR MUFFIN TIN

In most recipes, pans need just a quick coat of vegetable oil spray and they are ready to go. Try this trick to keep mess to a minimum.

Hold baking pan or muffin tin over sink. Spray inside of pan, making sure to get even coverage on bottom and sides. Don't worry if some spray misses the mark. It will wash off next time you wash dishes.

HOW TO GRATE OR SHRED CHEESE

Cheese is often cut into very small pieces to flavor pizza, bread, rolls, and more. When grating or shredding, use a big piece of cheese so your hand stays safely away from the sharp holes.

1. **To grate:** Hard cheeses such as Parmesan can be rubbed against a rasp grater or the small holes of a box grater to make a fluffy pile of cheese.

2. **To shred:** Semisoft cheeses such as cheddar or mozzarella can be rubbed against the large holes of a box grater to make long pieces of cheese.

HOW TO CHOP FRESH HERBS

Fresh herbs need to be washed and dried before they are chopped (or minced).

1. Use your fingers to remove leaves from stems; discard stems.

2. Gather leaves into small pile. Place one hand on handle of chef's knife and rest fingers of your other hand on top of blade. Use rocking motion, pivoting knife as you chop.

HOW TO ZEST AND JUICE CITRUS FRUIT

The flavorful colored skin from lemons, limes, and oranges (called the zest) is often removed and used in recipes. If you need zest, it's best to zest before juicing. After juicing, use a small spoon to remove any seeds from the bowl of juice.

1. **To zest:** Rub fruit against rasp grater to remove colored zest. Turn fruit as you rub to avoid bitter white layer underneath zest.

2. **To juice:** Cut fruit in half through equator (not through ends).

3. Place 1 half of fruit in citrus juicer. Hold juicer over bowl and squeeze to extract juice.

TOOLS MAKE THE WORK EASIER

The right gear is essential. You can't bake a layer cake in a loaf pan! Here are the tools you will use over and over again. We've divided items into six categories: knives, bakeware, kitchen basics, small appliances, prep tools, and baking tools. You will need some specialty items, such as a springform pan, tart pan, or small ramekins, for select recipes.

≡ KNIVES ≡

Paring knife

Chef's knife

Kid-friendly chef's knife

Cutting board

Bread knife

≈ BAKEWARE ≈

Rimmed baking sheet

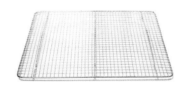

Cooling rack

12-cup and 24-cup muffin tins

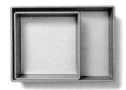

8-inch and 13-by-9-inch metal baking pans

9-inch round metal cake pan

8½-by-4½-inch metal loaf pan

9-inch pie plate

KITCHEN BASICS

Prep bowls

Oven mitts

Dish towels

Parchment paper

Aluminum foil

Plastic wrap

Toothpicks

SMALL APPLIANCES

Microwave

Blender

Food processor

Stand mixer

Electric handheld mixer

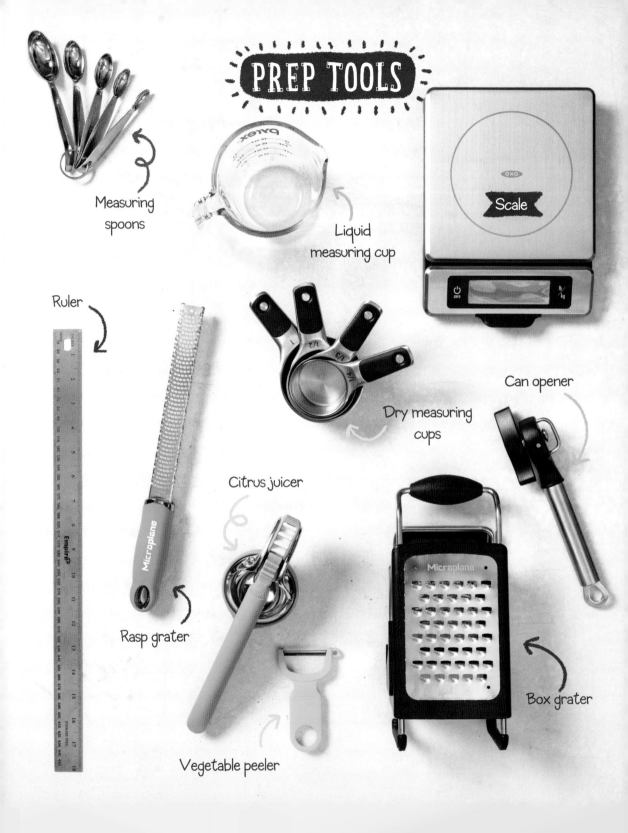

PREP TOOLS

Measuring spoons

Liquid measuring cup

Scale

Ruler

Dry measuring cups

Can opener

Citrus juicer

Rasp grater

Box grater

Vegetable peeler

BAKING TOOLS

Kid-friendly rolling pin
(see page 203)

Fine-mesh
strainer

Bench scraper

Icing spatula
(offset)

Spatula

Rubber
spatula

Whisk

Pastry
brush

Oven
thermometer

Instant-read
thermometer

For more information about
America's Test Kitchen Kids, visit
www.americastestkitchen.com/kids.

CHAPTER 1: MUFFINS, QUICK BREADS & OTHER BREAKFAST TREATS

WANT TO START YOUR DAY OFF RIGHT? OR MAKE A QUICK TREAT? LOOK NO FURTHER.

SPICED APPLESAUCE MUFFINS

MAKES 12 MUFFINS
TOTAL TIME: 55 MINUTES,
**   PLUS 25 MINUTES COOLING TIME**

PREPARE INGREDIENTS

Vegetable oil spray
¾ cup (3¾ ounces) all-purpose flour
¾ cup (4⅛ ounces) whole-wheat flour
1 teaspoon baking soda
½ teaspoon salt
⅔ cup (4⅔ ounces) sugar
½ teaspoon ground cinnamon
¼ teaspoon ground nutmeg
1 cup unsweetened applesauce
8 tablespoons unsalted butter,
    melted and cooled (see page 13
    for how to melt butter)
¼ cup (2 ounces) apple cider or apple juice
1 large egg
1 teaspoon vanilla extract

GATHER BAKING EQUIPMENT

12-cup muffin tin
3 bowls (1 large, 1 medium, 1 small)
Whisk
1-tablespoon measuring spoon
Rubber spatula
¼-cup dry measuring cup
Toothpick
Oven mitts
Cooling rack

"It was easy. It was so super delicious
that I made it twice." —Teagan, 12

START BAKING!

1. Adjust oven rack to middle position and heat oven to 375 degrees. Spray 12-cup muffin tin, including top, with vegetable oil spray.

2. In medium bowl, whisk together all-purpose flour, whole-wheat flour, baking soda, and salt.

3. In large bowl, whisk together sugar, cinnamon, and nutmeg. Transfer 2 tablespoons sugar mixture to small bowl and reserve for sprinkling.

4. Add applesauce, melted butter, cider, egg, and vanilla to remaining sugar mixture in large bowl and whisk until well combined.

5. Add flour mixture and use rubber spatula to gently stir until just combined and no dry flour is visible. Do not overmix (see page 38).

6. Spray ¼-cup dry measuring cup with vegetable oil spray. Use greased measuring cup to divide batter evenly among muffin cups (see photos, page 39). Sprinkle reserved sugar mixture evenly over batter in each muffin cup.

7. Place muffin tin in oven. Bake until muffins are deep golden brown and toothpick inserted in center of 1 muffin comes out clean (see photo, page 15), 20 to 25 minutes.

8. Use oven mitts to remove muffin tin from oven (ask an adult for help). Place muffin tin on cooling rack and let muffins cool in muffin tin for 15 minutes.

9. Using your fingertips, gently wiggle muffins to loosen from muffin tin (see photo, page 39) and transfer directly to cooling rack. Let muffins cool for at least 10 minutes before serving.

MUFFINS THAT TASTE LIKE FALL

It's always sad to say goodbye to the warm days of summer. But fall doesn't just mean back to school—it also means it's apple season! In baking, apples are often paired up with "warm" spices such as nutmeg and cinnamon. These spices aren't hot to the touch, but they can impart a sense of warmth because they are very full and aromatic. They are a great match for autumn produce such as apples, pumpkin, and squash. These muffins, full of applesauce, apple cider, cinnamon, and nutmeg, are tiny packages of fall flavors. Bonus: the sugar sprinkled on top gives them a sweet, crunchy crust!

BANANA AND CHOCOLATE CHIP MINI MUFFINS

MAKES 24 MINI MUFFINS
TOTAL TIME: 45 MINUTES,
   PLUS 20 MINUTES COOLING TIME

PREPARE INGREDIENTS

Vegetable oil spray
1⅓ cups (6⅔ ounces) all-purpose flour
½ teaspoon baking soda
¼ teaspoon salt
2 very ripe bananas (skins should be
   speckled black)
½ cup (3½ ounces) sugar
4 tablespoons unsalted butter,
   melted and cooled (see page 13
   for how to melt butter)
¼ cup plain yogurt
1 large egg
½ teaspoon vanilla extract
⅓ cup (2 ounces) mini chocolate chips

GATHER BAKING EQUIPMENT

24-cup mini
   muffin tin
2 bowls (1 large,
   1 medium)
Whisk
Large fork or
   potato masher

Rubber spatula
1-tablespoon
   measuring spoon
Toothpick
Oven mitts
Cooling rack

THE MANY SHADES OF BANANA

This recipe calls for very ripe bananas, which are sweeter and moister than underripe ones. To tell how ripe your banana is, look at the peel: If the peel looks greenish and feels a little hard, your banana is underripe. If it's bright yellow and a little bit soft, it's ripe (perfect for snacking!). And if it has black or brown spots and feels very soft, it's very ripe (great for baking). If you have too many very ripe bananas on hand, don't worry: freeze them to cook with later! Peel the bananas, place them in a zipper-lock bag, and put them in the freezer. Just thaw them before you bake.

START BAKING! ←《《《

1. Adjust oven rack to middle position and heat oven to 375 degrees. Spray 24-cup mini muffin tin well with vegetable oil spray (make sure to get inside each mini cup!).

2. In medium bowl, whisk together flour, baking soda, and salt.

3. Peel bananas and place in large bowl. Use large fork or potato masher to mash bananas until broken down but still chunky.

4. Add sugar, melted butter, yogurt, egg, and vanilla to bowl with bananas and whisk until combined.

5. Add flour mixture and chocolate chips and use rubber spatula to gently stir until just combined and no dry flour is visible. Batter should look thick and chunky—do not overmix (see page 38).

6. Spray 1-tablespoon measuring spoon with vegetable oil spray. Use greased measuring spoon to scoop 1 heaping tablespoon batter into each muffin tin cup (see photos, page 39).

7. Place muffin tin in oven. Bake until muffins are golden brown and toothpick inserted in center of 1 muffin comes out clean (see photo, page 15), 13 to 15 minutes.

8. Use oven mitts to remove muffin tin from oven (ask an adult for help). Place muffin tin on cooling rack and let muffins cool in muffin tin for 15 minutes.

9. Using your fingertips, gently wiggle muffins to loosen from muffin tin (see photo, page 39) and transfer directly to cooling rack. Let muffins cool for at least 5 minutes before serving.

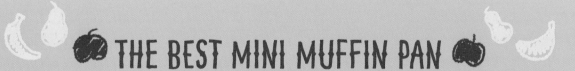

🍌 THE BEST MINI MUFFIN PAN 🍎

Tiny muffins are definitely cuter than large muffins. And do they taste better? Our unofficial, unscientific vote is yes! (Or maybe that's just because you can eat more than one in a sitting?) But to make mini muffins, you need a mini muffin pan. We tested mini muffin pans in the test kitchen and found that the **OXO Good Grips Non-Stick Pro 24-Cup Mini Muffin Pan ($24.99)** was our favorite. It released baked goods with ease (no sticking!), was easy to move in and out of the oven, and baked all of our muffins evenly. Mini muffins for all!

WHOLE-WHEAT RASPBERRY MUFFINS

MAKES 12 MUFFINS
TOTAL TIME: 55 MINUTES,
    PLUS 25 MINUTES COOLING TIME

PREPARE INGREDIENTS

Vegetable oil spray
3 cups (16½ ounces) whole-wheat flour
2½ teaspoons baking powder
½ teaspoon baking soda
1 teaspoon salt
2 large eggs
4 tablespoons unsalted butter,
    melted and cooled (see page 13
    for how to melt butter)
¼ cup vegetable oil
1 cup (7 ounces) sugar plus 2
    tablespoons sugar, measured
    separately
1¼ cups (10 ounces) buttermilk
1½ teaspoons vanilla extract
2 cups (10 ounces) fresh or frozen
    raspberries (do not thaw if frozen)

GATHER BAKING EQUIPMENT

12-cup muffin tin
2 bowls (1 large, 1 medium)
Whisk
Rubber spatula
⅓-cup dry measuring cup
Toothpick
Oven mitts
Cooling rack

"With the raspberries it's really good." —Catherine, 11

START BAKING!

1. Adjust oven rack to middle position and heat oven to 375 degrees. Spray 12-cup muffin tin, including top, with vegetable oil spray.

2. In medium bowl, whisk together flour, baking powder, baking soda, and salt.

3. In large bowl, whisk eggs, melted butter, oil, and 1 cup sugar until combined. Add buttermilk and vanilla to sugar mixture and whisk until well combined.

4. Add flour mixture and use rubber spatula to gently stir until just combined and no dry flour is visible. Gently stir raspberries into batter. Do not overmix (see page 38).

5. Spray ⅓-cup dry measuring cup with vegetable oil spray. Use greased measuring cup to divide batter evenly among muffin cups (see photos, page 39). Sprinkle remaining 2 tablespoons sugar evenly over batter.

6. Place muffin tin in oven. Bake until muffins are golden brown and toothpick inserted in center of 1 muffin comes out clean (see photo, page 15), 20 to 25 minutes.

7. Use oven mitts to remove muffin tin from oven (ask an adult for help). Place muffin tin on cooling rack and let muffins cool in muffin tin for 15 minutes.

8. Using your fingertips, gently wiggle muffins to loosen from muffin tin (see photo, page 39) and transfer directly to cooling rack. Let muffins cool for at least 10 minutes before serving.

BERRY, BERRY, QUITE CONTRARY

Did you know that even though raspberries are fruits, they are actually NOT berries?! Scientifically speaking, berries are fruits whose seeds and flesh come from just one flower. A single raspberry is actually made up of lots of tiny round fruits, each with its own seed. Therefore, a raspberry is called a composite fruit. Look at a raspberry up close or under a magnifying glass, and you can see the individual fruits. How cool is that?!

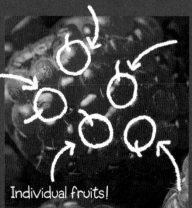

Individual fruits!

"Yum! Yum! Yum! Yum!
Delicious, scrumptious!"
—Dakota, 8

CORN MUFFINS

MAKES 12 MUFFINS
TOTAL TIME: 55 MINUTES,
  PLUS 25 MINUTES COOLING TIME

PREPARE INGREDIENTS

Vegetable oil spray
1½ cups (7½ ounces) all-purpose flour
1 cup (5 ounces) fine-ground, whole-
  grain yellow cornmeal
1½ teaspoons baking powder
1 teaspoon baking soda
½ teaspoon salt
½ cup (3½ ounces) sugar
2 large eggs
¾ cup sour cream
8 tablespoons unsalted butter,
  melted and cooled (see page 13
  for how to melt butter)
½ cup (4 ounces) whole milk

GATHER BAKING EQUIPMENT

12-cup muffin tin
2 bowls (1 large, 1 medium)
Whisk
Rubber spatula
¼-cup dry measuring cup
Toothpick
Oven mitts
Cooling rack

SO CORNY

Cornmeal is one of the most important ingredients made out of corn. It's used in everything from tortillas to polenta—and corn muffins! Cornmeal is made by milling dried corn kernels. The kernels are ground to one of three different sizes—coarse, medium, or fine. (We use the "fine" size in this recipe.) The type of corn used for cornmeal is called yellow dent corn, which is different from the sweet type of corn we eat off the cob and also different from the dried corn we pop and eat at the movies (that one, not surprisingly, is called popcorn).

START BAKING! ←‹‹‹‹‹

1. Adjust oven rack to middle position and heat oven to 375 degrees. Spray 12-cup muffin tin, including top, with vegetable oil spray.

2. In medium bowl, whisk together flour, cornmeal, baking powder, baking soda, and salt.

3. In large bowl, whisk sugar and eggs until well combined, light-colored, and thick, about 1 minute. Add sour cream, melted butter, and milk and whisk to combine.

4. Add flour mixture and use rubber spatula to gently stir until just combined and no dry flour is visible. Do not overmix (see page 38).

5. Spray ¼-cup dry measuring cup with vegetable oil spray. Use greased measuring cup to divide batter evenly among muffin cups (see photos, page 39).

6. Place muffin tin in oven. Bake until muffins are golden brown and tooth-pick inserted into center of 1 muffin comes out clean (see photo, page 15), 20 to 25 minutes.

7. Use oven mitts to remove muffin tin from oven (ask an adult for help). Place muffin tin on cooling rack and let muffins cool in muffin tin for 15 minutes.

8. Using your fingertips, gently wiggle muffins to loosen from muffin tin (see photo, page 39) and transfer directly to cooling rack. Let muffins cool for at least 10 minutes before serving.

ZUCCHINI BREAD

SERVES 10
TOTAL TIME: 1 HOUR AND 45 MINUTES,
  PLUS 1¼ HOURS COOLING TIME

PREPARE INGREDIENTS

Vegetable oil spray
1 cup (5½ ounces) whole-wheat flour
1 cup (5 ounces) all-purpose flour
1 teaspoon salt
1 teaspoon ground cinnamon
1 teaspoon baking powder
1 teaspoon baking soda
½ teaspoon ground nutmeg
1 cup packed (7 ounces) brown sugar
2 large eggs
¼ cup vegetable oil
1 teaspoon vanilla extract
1½ pounds zucchini (2 large zucchini)

GATHER BAKING EQUIPMENT

8½-by-4½-inch metal loaf pan
2 bowls (1 large, 1 medium)
Whisk
Chef's knife
Cutting board
Box grater
Dish towel
Rubber spatula
Toothpick
Oven mitts
Cooling rack

"I thought this recipe was fun to make and easy. I did not like having to squeeze out the zucchini water, but I still had fun because it was delicious and my family loved it." —Celeste, 9

THE SQUISH OF SQUASH

In this bread, zucchini tastes sweet and mild thanks to its costars cinnamon, nutmeg, brown sugar, and vanilla. The zucchini actually adds something very important to this bread: moisture! (After all, zucchini is about 95 percent water.) But there's a thin line between too little and too much moisture. (No one likes heavy, soggy zucchini bread.) This is why we squeeze out the extra water before adding the shredded zucchini to the batter.

START BAKING! ←≪≪≪

1. Adjust oven rack to middle position and heat oven to 325 degrees. Spray inside bottom and sides of 8½-by-4½-inch metal loaf pan with vegetable oil spray.

2. In medium bowl, whisk together whole-wheat flour, all-purpose flour, salt, cinnamon, baking powder, baking soda, and nutmeg.

3. In large bowl, whisk together brown sugar, eggs, oil, and vanilla.

4. Use chef's knife to trim off ends of zucchini. Shred zucchini on large holes of box grater and squeeze dry in dish towel (following photos, below). Transfer zucchini to bowl with brown sugar mixture. Use rubber spatula to stir until combined.

5. Add flour mixture and use rubber spatula to gently stir until just combined and no dry flour is visible. Do not overmix (see page 38).

6. Use rubber spatula to scrape batter into greased loaf pan and smooth top.

7. Place loaf pan in oven. Bake until zucchini bread is golden brown and toothpick inserted in center comes out clean (see photo, page 15), 1 hour and 5 minutes to 1¼ hours.

8. Use oven mitts to remove loaf pan from oven (ask an adult for help). Place loaf pan on cooling rack and let zucchini bread cool in pan for 15 minutes.

9. Use oven mitts to carefully turn loaf pan on its side and remove zucchini bread from pan. Let zucchini bread cool on cooling rack for at least 1 hour. Transfer to cutting board, slice, and serve.

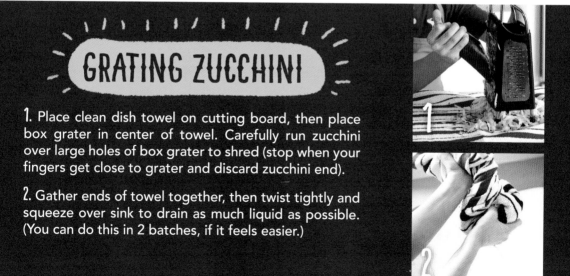

GRATING ZUCCHINI

1. Place clean dish towel on cutting board, then place box grater in center of towel. Carefully run zucchini over large holes of box grater to shred (stop when your fingers get close to grater and discard zucchini end).

2. Gather ends of towel together, then twist tightly and squeeze over sink to drain as much liquid as possible. (You can do this in 2 batches, if it feels easier.)

"I liked this recipe because I liked the whisking."
—Thomas, 10

"It reminded me of fall and Halloween. While I was cooking, the pumpkin smell was very mouthwatering!" —Ella, 11

PUMPKIN BREAD WITH CHOCOLATE CHIPS

SERVES 10
TOTAL TIME: 1 HOUR AND 50 MINUTES, PLUS 1¼ HOURS COOLING TIME

PREPARE INGREDIENTS

Vegetable oil spray
1¼ cups (6¼ ounces) all-purpose flour
1 teaspoon baking powder
½ teaspoon baking soda
2 large eggs
2 tablespoons (1 ounce) milk
¾ cup canned unsweetened pumpkin puree
¾ teaspoon ground cinnamon
½ teaspoon salt
⅛ teaspoon ground nutmeg
½ cup (3½ ounces) sugar
½ cup packed (3½ ounces) light brown sugar
½ cup vegetable oil
¾ cup (4½ ounces) chocolate chips

GATHER BAKING EQUIPMENT

8½-by-4½-inch metal loaf pan
2 bowls (1 medium, 1 small)
Whisk
Large saucepan
Rubber spatula
Toothpick
Oven mitts
Cooling rack
Cutting board
Chef's knife

START BAKING! ←⫷⫷⫷

1. Adjust oven rack to middle position and heat oven to 350 degrees. Spray inside bottom and sides of 8½-by-4½-inch metal loaf pan with vegetable oil spray.

2. In medium bowl, whisk together flour, baking powder, and baking soda. In small bowl, whisk together eggs and milk.

3. In large saucepan, combine pumpkin puree, cinnamon, salt, and nutmeg. Cook over medium heat, stirring constantly with rubber spatula, until mixture just begins to bubble, 4 to 6 minutes.

4. Turn off heat and slide saucepan to cool burner. Add sugar, brown sugar, and oil to pumpkin mixture and whisk until combined. Let mixture cool for 10 minutes. Whisk again until mixture is very smooth.

5. Add egg mixture to pumpkin mixture and whisk to combine. Add flour mixture and use rubber spatula to stir until just combined and no dry flour is visible. Stir chocolate chips into batter. Do not overmix (see page 38).

6. Use rubber spatula to scrape batter into greased loaf pan and smooth top. (Ask an adult for help because saucepan will be heavy.)

7. Place loaf pan in oven. Bake until toothpick inserted in center of pumpkin bread comes out clean (see photo, page 15), 50 minutes to 1 hour.

8. Use oven mitts to remove loaf pan from oven (ask an adult for help). Place loaf pan on cooling rack and let pumpkin bread cool in pan for 15 minutes.

9. Use oven mitts to carefully turn loaf pan on its side and remove pumpkin bread from pan. Let pumpkin bread cool on cooling rack for at least 1 hour. Transfer to cutting board, slice, and serve.

⸾⸾⸾⸾⸾ EVAPORATION NATION! ⸾⸾⸾⸾⸾

Quick breads should be moist but not soggy, so we often need to get rid of extra liquid in the batter. In our Zucchini Bread (page 32), we squeezed all the excess water out of the shredded zucchini to avoid a soggy loaf. We can't squeeze our pumpkin puree (that would be messy!), but cooking has the same effect. With heat, some of the water in the puree evaporates, helping keep the finished loaf moist but not soggy. As a bonus, cooking the puree takes away the raw pumpkin flavor and gives it some earthy caramel flavor. Add a little cinnamon and nutmeg and this bread smells (and tastes) like autumn. The chocolate chips turn this orange-and-black loaf into the perfect Halloween (trick-or-) treat!

QUICK CHEESE BREAD

SERVES 10
TOTAL TIME: 1 HOUR AND 20 MINUTES,
   PLUS 1¼ HOURS COOLING TIME

PREPARE INGREDIENTS

Vegetable oil spray
2½ cups (12½ ounces) all-purpose flour
1 tablespoon baking powder
½ teaspoon salt
⅛ teaspoon pepper (optional)
1 cup extra-sharp cheddar cheese cut
   into ¼-inch pieces (4 ounces)
½ cup shredded Parmesan cheese
   (1½ ounces) plus ½ cup shredded
   Parmesan cheese (1½ ounces),
   measured separately (see page 16
   for how to shred cheese)
1 cup (8 ounces) whole milk
½ cup sour cream
3 tablespoons unsalted butter, melted
   (see page 13 for how to melt butter)
1 large egg

GATHER BAKING EQUIPMENT

8½-by-4½-inch metal loaf pan
2 bowls (1 large, 1 medium)
Whisk
Rubber spatula
Toothpick
Oven mitts
Cooling rack
Cutting board
Chef's knife

"The cheese bread turned out soft, and there was
cheese in every bite. It was super-duper yummy.
   —Ethan, 10

"I thought it was very fun to make and it was the
perfect amount of challenging to make. I thought
it was delicious and amazing." —Sami, 11

1. Adjust oven rack to middle position and heat oven to 350 degrees. Spray inside bottom and sides of 8½-by-4½-inch metal loaf pan with vegetable oil spray.

2. In medium bowl, whisk together flour, baking powder, salt, and pepper (if using). Use rubber spatula to stir in cheddar cheese and ½ cup Parmesan cheese, breaking up clumps, until cheese is coated with flour.

3. In large bowl, whisk milk, sour cream, melted butter, and egg until well combined.

4. Add flour mixture and use rubber spatula to gently stir until just combined and no dry flour is visible. Batter will be heavy and thick—do not overmix (see page 38).

5. Use rubber spatula to scrape batter into greased loaf pan and smooth top. Sprinkle remaining ½ cup Parmesan cheese over batter.

6. Place loaf pan in oven. Bake until top of cheese bread is golden brown and toothpick inserted in center comes out clean (see photo, page 15), 45 to 55 minutes.

7. Use oven mitts to remove loaf pan from oven (ask an adult for help). Place loaf pan on cooling rack and let cheese bread cool in pan for 15 minutes.

8. Use oven mitts to carefully turn loaf pan on its side and remove cheese bread from pan. Let cheese bread cool on cooling rack for at least 1 hour. Transfer to cutting board, slice, and serve.

BRING ON THE CHEESE

We use two kinds of cheese in this quick bread to achieve maximum cheesiness. Shredded Parmesan adds a savory cheesy flavor throughout the loaf while cubes of cheddar cheese create ooey-gooey melted pockets in each and every slice. Topping the loaf with more shredded Parmesan gives the loaf a nice-looking and crunchy crust. Score!

WHEN IS IT DONE?

If, when you're testing for doneness, the toothpick comes out with what looks like uncooked batter clinging to it, try again in a different but still central spot. A toothpick hitting a pocket of cheese may give a false indication.

QUICK BREAD AND MUFFIN 101

Quick breads and muffins win the MVP award for baked goods. That's because not only are they delicious, but they are quick to make (and eat!).

WHAT IS A QUICK BREAD?

Most traditional bread recipes use yeast, which takes a long time to activate and grow inside the dough to help the bread rise (think hours and hours!). But "quick breads" are exactly that: breads that can be prepared and baked quickly. This is largely thanks to the power of baking powder and baking soda. These two ingredients are called chemical leaveners. When they're activated by liquid and either acid or heat during baking, they create carbon dioxide, a tasteless gas that helps baked goods rise—fast!

WHAT TO DO WITH LEFTOVERS

Most leftover muffins, biscuits, scones, and quick breads can be stored in a zipper-lock bag at room temperature for up to three days. When ready to serve, just refresh them by placing them on a baking sheet and warming them in a 300-degree oven for about 10 minutes.

Muffins and biscuits can also be frozen for up to one month. To freeze them, place muffins or biscuits in a single layer in a heavy-duty zipper-lock bag. To serve, thaw the muffins or biscuits at room temperature. To serve warm, heat the thawed muffins or biscuits in a 300-degree oven for about 10 minutes.

DON'T OVERMIX THE BATTER

To keep muffins, scones, and quick breads as light and tender as possible, the key is to not overmix the batter. This means mixing until just combined and the batter is not completely smooth. Why? The more you mix, the more the proteins in the flour combine to form gluten (see page 12 for more on gluten). The more gluten, the more structure and the tougher the quick bread. To prevent tough and squat breads, keep mixing to a minimum!

PORTIONING BATTER FOR MUFFINS

1. Spray measuring cup or measuring spoon needed for portioning in recipe with vegetable oil spray.

2. Scoop batter with greased measuring cup or spoon and scrape off any extra batter that is dripping from the bottom or overflowing on top. This ensures that all muffins will be equal in size and that there will be enough batter to fill all muffin tin cups.

3. Pour batter into muffin tin cup, using a rubber spatula to scrape batter from measuring cup or spoon if needed.

HOW TO REMOVE MUFFINS FROM THEIR TIN

Use your fingers to gently wiggle the muffins to help them easily slide out of the muffin tin. If they're still a little stuck, use a butter knife to carefully loosen the muffins from the muffin tin.

SIMPLE CREAM SCONES

MAKES 8 SCONES
TOTAL TIME: 40 MINUTES,
    PLUS 45 MINUTES COOLING TIME

PREPARE INGREDIENTS

2 cups (10 ounces) all-purpose flour
3 tablespoons sugar
1 tablespoon baking powder
½ teaspoon salt
5 tablespoons unsalted butter,
    cut into ¼-inch pieces and chilled
1 cup (8 ounces) heavy cream

GATHER BAKING EQUIPMENT

Rimmed baking sheet
Parchment paper
Food processor
Large bowl
Rubber spatula
Ruler
Bench scraper (or butter knife and spatula)
Oven mitts
Cooling rack

"The scones were very delicious,
moist, and flaky." —Victoria, 12

❤ BUTTERY GOODNESS ❤

They may be called cream scones, but a big part of the magic of these scones comes from the butter. Adding little pieces of cold butter to the flour mixture (with the help of the food processor) creates little pockets of butter in the dough. When the scones are baking, the water in that butter turns into steam. That steam creates little pockets of air, which help the scones turn out super flaky. (The cream is not for nothing: It makes the scones taste deliciously rich.) We like to serve these scones with our favorite jam (and sometimes even more butter...shh!).

START BAKING!

1. Adjust oven rack to middle position and heat oven to 425 degrees. Line rimmed baking sheet with parchment paper.

2. Place flour, sugar, baking powder, and salt in food processor. Lock lid into place. Turn on processor and process mixture for 3 seconds. Stop food processor.

3. Remove lid and sprinkle chilled butter over flour mixture. Lock lid back into place. Hold down pulse button for 1 second, then release. Repeat until mixture looks like coarse crumbs, about ten 1-second pulses. Remove lid and carefully remove processor blade (ask an adult for help).

4. Transfer flour-butter mixture to large bowl. Add cream and use rubber spatula to stir until just combined and no dry flour is visible. Do not overmix (see page 38).

5. Transfer mixture to clean counter and shape dough into 8 scones (following photos, right). Use bench scraper (or spatula) to transfer scones to parchment-lined baking sheet.

6. Place baking sheet in oven. Bake until scones are light brown on top, 10 to 14 minutes.

7. Use oven mitts to remove baking sheet from oven (ask an adult for help). Place baking sheet on cooling rack and let scones cool on baking sheet for 15 minutes.

8. Transfer scones directly to cooling rack. Let cool for 30 minutes before serving.

SHAPING SCONES

1. Transfer mixture to clean counter and use your hands to gather and press mixture until dough forms and holds together, 5 to 10 seconds.

2. Use your hands to pat dough into 8-inch circle, about ¾ inch thick.

3. Use bench scraper (or butter knife) to cut circle into 8 wedges.

BERRY SCONES

MAKES 8 SCONES
TOTAL TIME: 50 MINUTES,
    PLUS 45 MINUTES COOLING TIME

PREPARE INGREDIENTS

1 cup (5 ounces) frozen mixed berries
1 tablespoon confectioners' (powdered)
    sugar
1½ cups (7½ ounces) all-purpose flour,
    plus extra for counter
6 tablespoons unsalted butter, cut into
    ½-inch pieces and chilled
2 tablespoons sugar
1½ teaspoons baking powder
½ teaspoon salt
½ cup (4 ounces) whole milk
1 large egg yolk (see page 14
    for how to separate eggs)

GATHER BAKING EQUIPMENT

Rimmed baking sheet
Parchment paper
3 bowls (1 large, 2 medium)
Rubber spatula
Food processor
Whisk
Ruler
Bench scraper (or butter knife and spatula)
Oven mitts
Cooling rack

"They have a lot of flavor
and crunch on the bottom."
—Ben, 9

HOT TAKE: USE FROZEN FRUIT!

One key to flaky, tender scones is the ingredients you use, but another is the temperature of those ingredients. Using chilled butter—and mixing everything together quickly, before it warms up—helps create those perfect flaky layers. Using frozen berries helps keep the dough's temperature low. It also prevents the bright berry color from bleeding out of the berries and into the dough. If you don't like mixed berries, you can use 1 cup (5 ounces) of frozen raspberries, blueberries, or blackberries instead of the mixed berries.

START BAKING!

1. Adjust oven rack to upper-middle position and heat oven to 425 degrees. Line rimmed baking sheet with parchment paper.

2. In medium bowl, combine berries and confectioners' sugar. Use rubber spatula to stir to coat berries with confectioners' sugar. Place bowl in freezer until needed.

3. Place flour, chilled butter, sugar, baking powder, and salt in food processor. Lock lid in place. Hold down pulse button for 1 second, then release. Repeat until butter forms pea-size pieces, six to eight 1-second pulses.

4. Remove lid and carefully remove processor blade (ask an adult for help). Transfer flour mixture to large bowl. Use rubber spatula to stir in frozen berries until they are well coated.

5. In second medium bowl, whisk milk and egg yolk until well combined. Add milk mixture to flour mixture and use rubber spatula to stir until just combined into shaggy dough. Do not overmix (see page 38).

6. Sprinkle clean counter lightly with extra flour and coat your hands with flour. Transfer dough to floured counter and shape dough into 8 scones (following photos, page 41). Use bench scraper (or spatula) to transfer scones to parchment-lined baking sheet.

7. Place baking sheet in oven. Bake until scones are golden brown on top, about 14 minutes.

8. Use oven mitts to remove baking sheet from oven (ask an adult for help). Place baking sheet on cooling rack and let scones cool on baking sheet for 15 minutes.

9. Transfer scones directly to cooling rack. Let cool for 30 minutes before serving.

"It was delicious and crumbled and melted in my mouth. The flavors were very good, and in my opinion, it should be served with fruit and whipped cream." —Talia, 10

CRUMB CAKE

SERVES 16
TOTAL TIME: 1 HOUR AND 20 MINUTES, PLUS 1½ HOURS COOLING TIME

PREPARE INGREDIENTS

Crumb Topping
Vegetable oil spray
8 tablespoons unsalted butter, melted
   (see page 13 for how to melt butter)
⅓ cup packed (2⅓ ounces) dark brown sugar
¾ teaspoon ground cinnamon
⅓ cup (2⅓ ounces) sugar
⅛ teaspoon salt
1¾ cups (7 ounces) cake flour

Cake
¼ teaspoon baking soda
1¼ cups (5 ounces) cake flour
½ cup (3½ ounces) sugar
¼ teaspoon salt
6 tablespoons unsalted butter, cut into
   6 pieces and softened (see page 13
   for how to soften butter)
⅓ cup (2⅔ ounces) buttermilk
1 large egg plus 1 large yolk (see page 14
   for how to separate eggs)
1 teaspoon vanilla extract
1 to 2 teaspoons confectioners'
   (powdered) sugar

GATHER BAKING EQUIPMENT

Aluminum foil
Ruler
8-inch square metal baking pan
Medium bowl
Whisk
Rubber spatula
Electric mixer (stand mixer with paddle
   attachment or handheld mixer with large bowl)
Toothpick
Oven mitts
Cooling rack
Cutting board
Fine-mesh strainer
Chef's knife

CAKE FLOUR = TENDER CAKES

Remember: Protein in flour comes together during baking to form networks of gluten, which give structure to baked goods. More protein = more gluten = more structure. Compared to other flours, cake flour has the *least* amount of protein. And because we want a light and tender cake, we don't want a lot of structure. That means cake flour to the rescue!

START BAKING! ←《《《《

1. Adjust oven rack to upper-middle position and heat oven to 325 degrees. Make aluminum foil sling for 8-inch square metal baking pan (following photos, page 15). Spray foil lightly with vegetable oil spray.

2. **For the crumb topping:** In medium bowl, whisk together melted butter, brown sugar, cinnamon, ⅓ cup sugar, and ⅛ teaspoon salt. Add 1¾ cups flour and use rubber spatula to stir until mixture forms thick, uniform dough. Set aside.

3. **For the cake:** In bowl of stand mixer (or large bowl if using handheld mixer), combine baking soda, 1¼ cups flour, ½ cup sugar, and ¼ teaspoon salt. If using a stand mixer, lock bowl in place and attach paddle to stand mixer. Start mixer on low speed and mix until combined, about 5 seconds.

4. With mixer running, add softened butter, one piece at a time, and beat on low speed until mixture resembles coarse sand, about 1 minute. Stop mixer.

5. Add buttermilk, egg, egg yolk, and vanilla. Start mixer on low speed and beat until combined, about 20 seconds. Increase mixer speed to medium and beat until light and fluffy, about 2 minutes. Stop mixer and remove bowl from mixer, if using stand mixer.

6. Use rubber spatula to scrape down sides of bowl and stir in any remaining flour. Scrape batter into foil-lined baking pan and smooth top. Use your hands to break crumb topping dough into pea-size pieces. Sprinkle crumb topping in even layer over batter.

7. Place baking pan in oven. Bake until toothpick inserted in center of cake comes out clean (see photo, page 15), 35 to 45 minutes.

8. Use oven mitts to remove baking pan from oven (ask an adult for help). Place baking pan on cooling rack and let cake cool in pan for 30 minutes.

9. Use foil to lift cake out of baking pan and transfer to cooling rack. Let cake cool completely, about 1 hour. Transfer cake to cutting board.

10. Dust cake with confectioners' sugar (following photos, page 217). Cut cake into squares and serve.

> "The outside is good. They smell delicious. I want another one—I'm gonna pop it in my mouth!"
> —Oliver, 10

MINI MUFFIN TIN DOUGHNUT HOLES

MAKES 24 DOUGHNUT HOLES
TOTAL TIME: 50 MINUTES,
   PLUS 10 MINUTES COOLING TIME

PREPARE INGREDIENTS

Doughnuts
Vegetable oil spray
1⅓ cups (6⅔ ounces) all-purpose flour
2 tablespoons cornstarch
1½ teaspoons baking powder
½ teaspoon salt
¼ teaspoon ground nutmeg
½ cup (3½ ounces) sugar
½ cup (4 ounces) buttermilk
4 tablespoons unsalted butter, melted
   (see page 13 for how to melt butter)
1 large egg plus 1 large yolk (see page 14
   for how to separate eggs)

Topping
4 tablespoons unsalted butter
1 teaspoon ground cinnamon
½ cup (3½ ounces) sugar

GATHER BAKING EQUIPMENT

24-cup mini muffin tin
4 bowls (1 large, 2 medium,
   1 small microwave-safe)
Whisk
Rubber spatula
1-tablespoon measuring spoon
Toothpick
Oven mitts
Cooling rack
Rimmed baking sheet
Pastry brush

START BAKING! ←—≪≪≪

1. **For the doughnuts:** Adjust oven rack to middle position and heat oven to 400 degrees. Spray 24-cup mini muffin tin well with vegetable oil spray.

2. In medium bowl, whisk together flour, cornstarch, baking powder, salt, nutmeg, and ½ cup sugar.

3. In large bowl, whisk buttermilk, 4 tablespoons melted butter, egg, and egg yolk until well combined.

4. Add flour mixture and use rubber spatula to stir until just combined and no dry flour is visible. Do not overmix (see page 38).

5. Spray 1-tablespoon measuring spoon with vegetable oil spray. Use greased measuring spoon to scoop 1 tablespoon batter into each muffin tin cup (see photos, page 39).

6. Place muffin tin in oven. Bake until toothpick inserted in center of 1 doughnut hole comes out clean (see photo, page 15), about 10 minutes.

7. Use oven mitts to remove muffin tin from oven (ask an adult for help). Place muffin tin on cooling rack and let doughnut holes cool in muffin tin for 10 minutes.

8. **For the topping:** In small microwave-safe bowl, melt remaining 4 tablespoons butter. In second medium bowl, use clean rubber spatula to stir together cinnamon and remaining ½ cup sugar.

9. Carefully remove doughnut holes from muffin tin and transfer directly to cooling rack (ask an adult for help—muffin tin will be hot). Place cooling rack in rimmed baking sheet. Use pastry brush to paint doughnut holes all over with melted butter (use all of butter). Then, roll each doughnut hole in cinnamon sugar to coat all over. Serve.

 ## WHY DO DOUGHNUTS HAVE HOLES?

Rumor has it that a ship captain in the mid-1800s was the first to create ring-shaped doughnuts with holes in the centers. Some say he did it so he could keep them skewered on the spikes of his ship's wheel and snack while steering! Whatever the reason, most doughnuts have holes. And for almost as long as there have been doughnuts, bakers have been turning the dough removed from the centers into doughnut holes. We wanted to make doughnut holes…but without the rest of the doughnut. A muffin tin made it easy. And brushing the doughnut holes with melted butter after baking and then rolling them in cinnamon sugar while they were still warm gave them a delicious, sweet coating.

> "I like the outside—it has a crispy outside and tender inside."
> —Elizabeth, 10

POPOVERS

MAKES 10 POPOVERS
TOTAL TIME: 2 HOURS AND 10 MINUTES,
PLUS 10 MINUTES COOLING TIME

PREPARE INGREDIENTS

2 cups (11 ounces) bread flour
1 teaspoon salt
1 teaspoon sugar
3 large eggs
2 cups (16 ounces) low-fat milk
3 tablespoons unsalted butter,
   cut into 3 pieces
Vegetable oil spray

GATHER BAKING EQUIPMENT

3 bowls (1 large, 1 medium, 1 medium microwave-safe)
Whisk
Oven mitts
Large liquid measuring cup
Plastic wrap
12-cup muffin tin
Toothpick
Cooling rack

START BAKING!

1. In medium bowl, whisk together flour, salt, and sugar. In large bowl, whisk eggs until foamy and light-colored, about 1 minute. Set aside both bowls.

2. In medium microwave-safe bowl, combine milk and butter. Heat in microwave at 50 percent power (see page 11) for 1 minute and 30 seconds. Stop microwave and use clean whisk to stir mixture. Heat in microwave at 50 percent power until butter is melted, about 1 minute and 30 seconds. Use oven mitts to remove bowl from microwave.

3. Pour milk mixture into bowl with eggs and whisk until well combined.

4. Add flour mixture and whisk until smooth and no lumps of flour remain. Transfer batter to large liquid measuring cup. Cover measuring cup with plastic wrap and let sit at room temperature for 1 hour.

5. While batter sits, adjust oven rack to lower-middle position and heat oven to 450 degrees. Spray 12-cup muffin tin, including top, with vegetable oil spray.

6. After batter has sat for 1 hour, whisk batter to recombine, then pour into outer 10 muffin tin cups, leaving 2 middle cups empty (batter will not quite reach tops of cups).

7. Place muffin tin in oven. Bake popovers for 12 minutes. Without opening oven door, reduce oven temperature to 300 degrees and continue to bake for 20 minutes.

8. Open oven door, use oven mitts to pull out oven rack, and use toothpick to poke small hole in top of each popover (ask an adult for help) (see photo, right). Return popovers to oven and bake until deep golden brown, 8 to 10 minutes.

9. Use oven mitts to remove muffin tin from oven (ask an adult for help). Place muffin tin on cooling rack. Use toothpick to poke each popover again and let cool in muffin tin for 5 minutes. Using your fingertips, gently wiggle popovers to loosen from muffin tin (see photo, page 39) and transfer directly to cooling rack. Serve warm.

POPPING POPOVERS

Use a toothpick to poke a small hole in the top of each popover (ask an adult for help). These small holes allow the steam that helped pop up the popovers to escape (and keep them from collapsing and shriveling up when they come out of the oven).

POP RIGHT OVER

The name says it all—as popover batter bakes in the oven, it rises in the muffin tin (or special popover pan) and pops over the tops of the muffin tin cups. To make sure they pop, we use bread flour, which has a high protein content. The protein gives the popovers structure and helps them rise extra high. We recommend using King Arthur bread flour, which has more protein than most other super-market bread flours. If you can't find King Arthur, another bread flour will work, but your popovers might not be quite as tall.

BUTTERMILK BISCUITS

MAKES 12 BISCUITS
TOTAL TIME: 1 HOUR,
 PLUS 15 MINUTES COOLING TIME

PREPARE INGREDIENTS

Dough
Vegetable oil spray
1 tablespoon baking powder
½ teaspoon baking soda
1 tablespoon sugar
1 teaspoon salt
2 cups (10 ounces) all-purpose flour
4 tablespoons unsalted butter, cut into
 ¼-inch pieces and chilled
1½ cups (12 ounces) buttermilk, chilled

To Form and Bake Biscuits
1 cup (5 ounces) all-purpose flour
2 tablespoons unsalted butter,
 melted and cooled (see page 13
 for how to melt butter)

GATHER BAKING EQUIPMENT

9-inch round metal cake pan
Food processor
Medium bowl
Rubber spatula
Rimmed baking sheet
¼-cup dry measuring cup
Pastry brush
Oven mitts
Cooling rack

"Maybe the best biscuits ever!" —Alex, 9

"I had to read through the directions a few times,
but they turned out really good." —Jack, 13

START BAKING! ←≪≪

1. **For the dough:** Adjust oven rack to middle position and heat oven to 450 degrees. Spray inside bottom and sides of 9-inch round metal cake pan with vegetable oil spray.

2. Place baking powder, baking soda, sugar, salt, and 2 cups flour in food processor. Lock lid into place. Hold down pulse button for 1 second, then release. Repeat until ingredients are combined, about six 1-second pulses.

3. Remove lid and scatter chilled butter pieces evenly over flour mixture. Lock lid back into place. Pulse until mixture resembles pebbly, coarse cornmeal, eight to ten 1-second pulses.

4. Remove lid and carefully remove food processor blade (ask an adult for help). Transfer flour mixture to medium bowl. Add buttermilk and use rubber spatula to gently stir until just combined and no dry flour is visible. Do not overmix (see page 38).

5. **To form and bake biscuits:** Sprinkle remaining 1 cup flour evenly over rimmed baking sheet. Spray ¼-cup dry measuring cup with vegetable oil spray. Use greased measuring cup to scoop batter and use rubber spatula to scrape off extra batter. Drop scoops onto floured baking sheet to make 12 biscuits (use rubber spatula to scrape dough from measuring cup if needed).

6. Use flour from baking sheet to flour your hands. Working with 1 piece of dough at a time, flour and shape dough and transfer to greased cake pan (following photos, below).

7. Use pastry brush to paint tops of dough rounds with melted butter.

8. Place cake pan in oven. Bake until biscuits are deep golden brown, about 20 minutes.

9. Use oven mitts to remove cake pan from oven (ask an adult for help). Place cake pan on cooling rack and let biscuits cool in pan for 15 minutes. Turn cake pan upside down to release biscuits from pan. Turn biscuits right side up and use your hands to pull them apart. Serve warm.

SHAPING FLUFFY BISCUITS

1. Working with 1 piece of dough at a time, use your hands to roll piece of dough in flour until evenly coated.

2. Gently pick up dough piece, shape into rough ball, and shake off excess flour.

3. Place dough ball in cake pan so it is touching edge of pan. Repeat with remaining dough pieces, arranging 9 rounds around edge of pan and 3 rounds in center.

CHERRY, ALMOND, AND CHOCOLATE CHIP GRANOLA

MAKES 5 CUPS
TOTAL TIME: 1 HOUR AND 10 MINUTES,
**   PLUS 45 MINUTES COOLING TIME**

"It's a great movie night snack!" —Caroline, 9

"It's crunchy and just the right amount
of sweetness." —Elise, 11

PREPARE INGREDIENTS

Vegetable oil spray
¼ cup vegetable oil
3 tablespoons maple syrup
2 tablespoons packed light brown
    sugar
2 teaspoons vanilla extract
¼ teaspoon salt
2½ cups (7½ ounces) old-fashioned
    rolled oats
1 cup sliced almonds
1 cup dried cherries
½ cup (3 ounces) semisweet chocolate
    chips

GATHER BAKING EQUIPMENT

13-by-9-inch metal baking pan
2 bowls (1 large, 1 medium)
Rubber spatula
Oven mitts
Cooling rack
Butter knife

1. Adjust oven rack to middle position and heat oven to 325 degrees. Spray inside bottom and sides of 13-by-9-inch metal baking pan with vegetable oil spray.

2. In large bowl, combine oil, maple syrup, brown sugar, vanilla, and salt and use rubber spatula to stir until well combined. Stir in oats and almonds until combined.

3. Transfer oat mixture to greased baking pan and use rubber spatula to spread mixture into even layer. Use rubber spatula to press down firmly on oat mixture until mixture is very flat (see photo, right).

4. Place baking pan in oven. Bake until lightly browned, 35 to 40 minutes.

5. Use oven mitts to remove baking pan from oven (ask an adult for help). Place baking pan on cooling rack and let granola cool completely in pan, about 45 minutes.

6. Use butter knife to crack granola into large pieces. Then, use your hands to break cooled granola into bite-size pieces. Transfer granola to medium bowl. Use rubber spatula to stir in cherries and chocolate chips. Serve. (Granola can be stored in airtight container for up to 2 weeks.)

MAKE IT YOUR WAY

Granola is a naturally gluten-free power breakfast. Feel free to swap in your favorite nuts, seeds, and dried fruits. Or try our Superpower Granola!

SUPERPOWER GRANOLA

Reduce rolled oats to 1½ cups. Add 1 cup quinoa flakes with oats and almonds in step 2. Use 1 cup dried cranberries instead of dried cherries and use ½ cup raw sunflower seeds instead of mini chocolate chips in step 6.

PACK YOUR GRANOLA

The key to getting big, crunchy bites is to pack the oat mixture into the pan before you bake it. Use rubber spatula to spread mixture into even layer. Use rubber spatula to press down firmly on oat mixture until mixture is very flat.

CHAPTER 2: YEAST BREADS

NOW YOU, TOO, CAN MAKE BREAD LIKE YOU BUY IN THE BAKERY! IT'S ALL THANKS TO THE POWER OF YEAST.

EASY WHOLE-WHEAT SANDWICH BREAD

MAKES 1 LOAF
TOTAL TIME: 1¼ HOURS, PLUS 30 MINUTES RISING TIME, PLUS 3¼ HOURS COOLING TIME

PREPARE INGREDIENTS

Vegetable oil spray
1½ cups (8¼ ounces) whole-wheat flour
1 cup (5½ ounces) bread flour
2¼ teaspoons instant or rapid-rise yeast
1 teaspoon salt
1¼ cups plus 2 tablespoons (11 ounces)
    warm water
2 tablespoons unsalted butter, melted
    (see page 13 for how to melt butter)
1 tablespoon honey
1 large egg, cracked into bowl and
    lightly beaten with fork (see page 14)

GATHER BAKING EQUIPMENT

8½-by-4½-inch metal loaf pan
Stand mixer with paddle attachment
Whisk
4-cup liquid measuring cup
Rubber spatula
Ruler
Pastry brush
Oven mitts
Cooling rack
Butter knife
Cutting board
Bread knife

"It's pretty simple to make. The crust is just the right toughness, and the bread tastes delicious! I definitely want to make this bread again!" —Aidan, 9

START BAKING! ←—≪≪≪

1. Spray inside bottom and sides of 8½-by-4½-inch metal loaf pan with vegetable oil spray.

2. In bowl of stand mixer, whisk together whole-wheat flour, bread flour, yeast, and salt. Lock bowl in place and attach paddle to stand mixer. In 4-cup liquid measuring cup, whisk warm water, melted butter, and honey until honey has dissolved.

3. Start mixer on low speed. Slowly pour water mixture into flour mixture and mix until batter comes together, about 1 minute. Increase speed to medium and knead dough for 5 minutes. (Dough will look smooth and wet, almost like cake batter.) Stop mixer.

4. Spray rubber spatula with vegetable oil spray. Use greased spatula to transfer batter to greased loaf pan. Use spatula to push dough into corners of loaf pan and spread into even layer. Spray top of dough lightly with vegetable oil spray. Let dough rise, uncovered, until dough is about ½ inch above top edge of loaf pan (see photo, right), 30 minutes to 1 hour.

5. While dough rises, adjust oven rack to middle position and heat oven to 375 degrees. Just before baking, use pastry brush to gently paint top of dough with beaten egg.

6. Place loaf pan in oven. Bake until bread is deep golden brown, 40 to 45 minutes.

7. Use oven mitts to remove loaf pan from oven (ask an adult for help). Place loaf pan on cooling rack and let bread cool in pan for 15 minutes.

8. Carefully run butter knife around edges of bread to loosen from loaf pan (ask an adult for help—pan will be hot). Use oven mitts to carefully turn loaf pan on its side and remove bread from pan. Let bread cool completely on cooling rack, about 3 hours. Transfer bread to cutting board, slice (ask an adult for help), and serve.

BREAD IN A FLASH!

Most sandwich breads take a whole day to make! But this recipe comes together so fast for a few reasons: We use high-protein bread flour to give the loaf good structure. We add a lot of water so the dough can be poured into the pan (no kneading). And, we use a lot of yeast to help the dough rise fast as lightning!

LET IT RISE IN THE PAN

Let dough rise, uncovered, until dough is about ½ inch above top edge of loaf pan, 30 minutes to 1 hour. Be careful not to let the dough sit much longer than 1 hour. It can overproof, which means it will collapse in the oven.

ALMOST NO-KNEAD BREAD

MAKES 1 LOAF
TOTAL TIME: 2 HOURS AND 40 MINUTES,
   PLUS 9½ HOURS RISING TIME,
   PLUS 3 HOURS COOLING TIME

PREPARE INGREDIENTS

3 cups (15 ounces) all-purpose flour, plus
   extra for counter
2 teaspoons salt
¼ teaspoon instant or rapid-rise yeast
1 cup plus 2 tablespoons
   (9 ounces) room-temperature water
1 tablespoon distilled white vinegar
Vegetable oil spray

GATHER BAKING EQUIPMENT

Day 1
Large bowl
Whisk
Rubber spatula
Plastic wrap

Day 2
Ruler
Parchment paper
Small Dutch oven with lid
Oven mitts
Cooling rack
Cutting board
Bread knife

SEE YA, KNEADING!

Most breads require kneading the dough a long time to develop gluten, a stretchy web of proteins that gives bread its structure. But gluten can also develop on its own...with time. After a brief mix (see photo, right), letting our dough rest overnight (also called autolysis) lets the flour slowly form networks of gluten—just a quick knead the next day, and it's ready to bake.

START BAKING!

1. **Day 1:** In large bowl, whisk together flour, salt, and yeast. Add water and vinegar. Use rubber spatula to stir and press until dough comes together and no dry flour is visible, 2 to 3 minutes (see photo, left).

2. Cover bowl with plastic wrap and let dough rise until bubbly and doubled in size, at least 8 hours or up to 18 hours.

3. **Day 2:** Lay 18-by-12-inch sheet of parchment paper on counter. Spray parchment lightly with vegetable oil spray. Set aside.

4. Sprinkle clean counter heavily with extra flour and coat your hands with extra flour. Transfer dough to counter and use your floured hands to knead until smooth (see photos, page 61), about 1 minute. Move dough to clean portion of counter. Use your hands to form dough into smooth ball.

5. Transfer ball to center of greased parchment sheet. Use parchment to lower dough into Dutch oven (let any extra parchment hang over pot edges). Cover pot with lid and let dough rise until doubled in size, 1½ to 2 hours.

6. Adjust oven rack to middle position. When dough is ready, place covered pot in cold oven. Set oven to 425 degrees and bake for 30 minutes.

7. Ask an adult to remove pot lid with oven mitts (lid will be VERY hot). Continue to bake until loaf is deep golden brown, 20 to 25 minutes.

8. Ask an adult to remove pot from oven and to carefully lift parchment and bread out of pot and transfer to cooling rack (pot will be VERY hot). Let bread cool completely on cooling rack, about 3 hours. Transfer bread to cutting board, discard parchment, slice (ask an adult for help), and serve.

YEAST BREAD 101

Bread is magical. A simple combination of flour, water, and yeast (plus or minus a few things) comes together, with a bit of kneading and a little time, to create crusty, craggy, sliceable, toastable, delicious bread!

STEP BY STEP: BREAD BAKING

Every yeasted bread is different, but almost all yeasted breads follow the same basic steps to go from raw flour to finished loaves or rolls.

1. MIX
First, combine the dry and wet ingredients.

2. KNEAD
Then, develop the gluten structure (see right) through mixing and kneading, either with your hands or a stand mixer.

3. RISE
Let the yeast do its magic! The yeast creates gas bubbles that cause the bread to expand and develop flavor.

4. SHAPE
If needed, form the risen dough into shapes such as rolls or pretzels.

5. SECOND RISE
The dough needs time to rise again after it's been shaped.

6. BAKE
In the oven, the dough will turn into bread! It rises one last time in the hot oven (this is called oven spring) while it bakes through.

WHAT TO DO WITH LEFTOVER BREAD

Cooled bread can be wrapped in plastic wrap and stored at room temperature for up to 2 days. To reheat focaccia and za'atar bread, place bread on baking sheet and refresh in 325-degree oven for 5 minutes.

WATER, WATER EVERYWHERE!

One of the key ingredients in bread is flour, of course. But water is just as important! This is because gluten can't be created without water. More water = more gluten = more structure in your bread. (Up to a point— too much water, and it will just be a soggy loaf!) This is why many bakers spend a lot of time thinking about how much water they have in their bread in relation to how much flour. The calculation of hydration in a bread is called a baker's percentage. We won't calculate any percentages in this book, but we do think it's important to weigh the water in your recipes to make sure you have exactly the right amount. (See page 10 for more on measuring and weighing ingredients.)

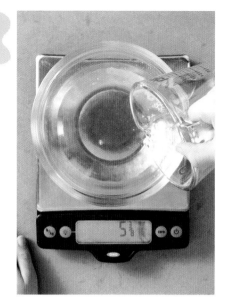

KNEADING AND SHAPING DOUGH INTO A SMOOTH BALL

1. Place heel of your hand in center of dough ball and press down and away from you.

2. Fold dough over. Rotate dough and repeat steps 1 & 2 until dough looks smooth, about 1 minute.

3. On clean counter, use your cupped hands to drag dough in small circles to form smooth ball.

ROMAN-STYLE FOCACCIA

SERVES 8
TOTAL TIME: 1¼ HOURS, PLUS 2 HOURS RISING
TIME, PLUS 15 MINUTES COOLING TIME

PREPARE INGREDIENTS

Dough
3 cups (15 ounces) all-purpose flour
1½ teaspoons instant or rapid-rise yeast
1½ teaspoons sugar
1⅔ cups (13½ ounces) room-temperature
  water
1½ teaspoons kosher salt
2 tablespoons extra-virgin olive oil

To Finish and Bake
Vegetable oil spray
2 tablespoons extra-virgin olive oil
2 tablespoons fresh rosemary leaves
1 teaspoon kosher salt

GATHER BAKING EQUIPMENT

Stand mixer with paddle attachment
Whisk
Rubber spatula
Large bowl
Pastry brush
Plastic wrap
13-by-9-inch metal baking pan
Fork
Oven mitts
Cooling rack
Spatula
Cutting board
Bread knife

→ ALL DOUGHS LEAD TO ROME ←

Pizza bianca (which means "white pizza" in Italian) is a popular snack sold at bakeries in Rome. This type of pizza might seem a little strange at first because it isn't topped with any tomato sauce or cheese, but trust us, it's delicious! Traditionally, pizza bianca is baked directly on the "floor" (or the stone bottom) of a pizza oven and is lightly charred, bubbly, and mostly flat. For our version, we bake the dough in a baking pan, which makes it puff up like another Italian specialty, focaccia. So think of this recipe as a pizza bianca–focaccia mash-up. *Buon appetito!*

1. **For the dough:** In bowl of stand mixer, whisk together flour, yeast, and sugar. Lock bowl in place and attach paddle to stand mixer.

2. Add water to mixer bowl, start mixer on low speed, and mix until no dry flour is visible, 3 to 4 minutes (stop mixer every 1 to 2 minutes and use rubber spatula to scrape down sides and bottom of bowl). Stop mixer and let dough sit for 10 minutes.

3. Add 1½ teaspoons salt to mixer bowl. Start mixer on low speed and mix until combined, about 30 seconds. Increase speed to medium-high and knead dough for 8 minutes. (Dough will look shiny, smooth, and very wet, almost like cake batter.) Stop mixer.

4. Pour 2 tablespoons oil into large bowl. Use pastry brush to evenly coat sides of bowl with oil. Use rubber spatula to transfer dough to bowl with oil. Use rubber spatula and your hands to flip dough to evenly coat with oil. Wash your hands. Cover bowl with plastic wrap. Let dough rise until bubbly and nearly tripled in size, 2 to 2½ hours.

5. **To finish and bake:** While dough rises, adjust oven rack to middle position and heat oven to 450 degrees. Spray inside bottom and sides of 13-by-9-inch metal baking pan with vegetable oil spray. Pour remaining 2 tablespoons oil into baking pan and use pastry brush to evenly coat pan with oil.

6. When dough is ready, use rubber spatula to transfer dough to greased baking pan. Use your fingertips to gently pat and stretch dough out to corners of baking pan. (If dough snaps back when you press it to corners of baking pan, cover it with plastic wrap, let it rest for 10 minutes, and try again.)

7. Let dough sit for 10 minutes. Use fork to lightly poke surface of dough all over about 20 times (this releases any big bubbles in dough). Sprinkle rosemary and remaining 1 teaspoon salt evenly over dough.

8. Place baking pan in oven and bake until focaccia is golden brown, 20 to 25 minutes.

9. Use oven mitts to remove baking pan from oven (ask an adult for help). Place baking pan on cooling rack and let focaccia cool in pan for 15 minutes.

10. Use spatula to transfer focaccia to cutting board. Cut into pieces (ask an adult for help) and serve.

MIDDLE EASTERN ZA'ATAR BREAD

SERVES 10 TO 12
TOTAL TIME: 1¼ HOURS, PLUS 2 HOURS RISING
  TIME, PLUS 15 MINUTES COOLING TIME

PREPARE INGREDIENTS

Dough
Vegetable oil spray
2 tablespoons plus 2 tablespoons
  extra-virgin olive oil, measured separately
1⅓ cups (10⅔ ounces) ice water (see page 11
  for how to measure ice water)
3½ cups (19¼ ounces) bread flour
2½ teaspoons instant or rapid-rise yeast
2½ teaspoons sugar
2 teaspoons salt

To Finish and Bake
¼ cup za'atar spice blend
¼ cup extra-virgin olive oil

GATHER BAKING EQUIPMENT

Rimmed baking sheet
Pastry brush
Liquid measuring cup
Food processor
Plastic wrap
Small bowl
Spoon
Oven mitts

Cooling rack
Spatula
Cutting board
Pizza wheel or chef's knife

"It was interesting to have something
called za'atar bread." —Jake, 8

"The seasoning has a good taste—
a little tiny bit lemony." —Joel, 10

START BAKING!

1. **For the dough:** Spray rimmed baking sheet with vegetable oil spray. Pour 2 tablespoons oil over baking sheet and use pastry brush to evenly coat baking sheet with oil.

2. In liquid measuring cup, combine ice water and next 2 tablespoons oil.

3. Add flour, yeast, and sugar to food processor and lock lid into place. Hold down pulse button for 1 second, then release. Repeat until ingredients are combined, about five 1-second pulses.

4. Turn on processor, then slowly pour water mixture through feed tube and process until dough comes together and no dry flour remains, about 30 seconds.

5. Stop processor. Let dough sit for 10 minutes. Add salt to processor and process for 1 minute.

KEEP GOING! »»»→

ZIPPY ZA'ATAR

Za'atar, a spice blend used frequently in Middle Eastern cuisine, usually consists of dried wild thyme, ground sumac (a tart, fruity spice), and sesame seeds. Some versions of za'atar also use dried oregano and salt. This spice blend can be used in a lot of different ways—sprinkled over meat or fish or mixed with olive oil for dipping bread. This recipe is inspired by *mana'eesh*, a round Arabic flatbread covered with a thick coating of za'atar and olive oil. It makes for a delicious breakfast or snack, especially when served with Greek yogurt or *labneh* (a very thick Middle Eastern yogurt) for dipping.

6. Stop processor, remove lid, and carefully remove processor blade (ask an adult for help). Lightly spray clean counter and your hands with vegetable oil spray. Transfer dough to greased counter and use your hands to knead dough for 30 seconds (see photos 1 and 2, page 61).

7. Place dough on oiled baking sheet and turn to coat with oil on both sides. Cover loosely with plastic wrap. Let dough rise until bubbly and nearly tripled in size, 2 to 2½ hours.

8. To finish and bake: While dough rises, adjust oven rack to lower-middle position and heat oven to 375 degrees. In small bowl, use spoon to stir together za'atar and remaining ¼ cup oil.

9. When dough is ready, use your hands to gently press down on dough to pop any large bubbles. Shape and top dough (following photos, right).

10. Place baking sheet in oven. Bake bread until edges are crisp and golden brown, 20 to 25 minutes.

11. Use oven mitts to remove baking sheet from oven (ask an adult for help). Place baking sheet on cooling rack and let bread cool in baking sheet for 15 minutes.

12. Use spatula to loosen edges of bread, then carefully slide bread onto cutting board. Use pizza wheel or chef's knife to cut bread into pieces. Serve.

SHAPING ZA'ATAR BREAD

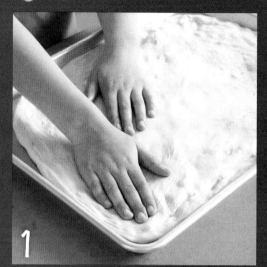

1. Use your hands to gently pat and stretch dough out to corners of baking sheet. (If dough snaps back when you press it to corners of baking sheet, cover it with plastic wrap, let it rest for 10 minutes, and try again.)

2. Use your fingertips to dimple entire surface of dough.

3. Spoon za'atar-oil mixture over dough and use back of spoon to spread into even layer all the way to edge of dough.

FLUFFY DINNER ROLLS

MAKES 9 ROLLS
TOTAL TIME: 1 HOUR AND 20 MINUTES,
   PLUS 2½ HOURS RISING TIME,
   PLUS 30 MINUTES COOLING TIME

PREPARE INGREDIENTS

2½ cups (12½ ounces) all-purpose flour
2¼ teaspoons instant or rapid-rise yeast
1 teaspoon salt
¾ cup (6 ounces) room-temperature
   whole milk
4 tablespoons unsalted butter, melted
   (see page 13 for how to melt butter)
2 tablespoons honey
1 large egg yolk (see page 14 for how to
   separate eggs)
Vegetable oil spray
1 large egg, cracked into bowl and lightly
   beaten with fork (see page 14)

GATHER BAKING EQUIPMENT

Stand mixer with dough hook attachment
Whisk
4-cup liquid measuring cup
2 bowls (1 large, 1 small)
Plastic wrap
Ruler
Bench scraper (or kitchen shears)

8-inch square metal baking pan
Pastry brush
Oven mitts
Cooling rack

START BAKING!

"My favorite part was kneading and shaping the dough. It was like playing with slime." —Morgan, 11

"I loved the recipe because it was my first time baking, so it was a good start for baking. And when I tried it, it was great." —Maya, 9

1. In bowl of stand mixer, whisk together flour, yeast, and salt. Lock bowl in place and attach dough hook to stand mixer.

2. In 4-cup liquid measuring cup, whisk milk, melted butter, honey, and egg yolk until honey has dissolved, about 20 seconds.

3. Start mixer on low speed and slowly pour in milk mixture. Mix until no dry flour is visible, about 2 minutes. Increase speed to medium and knead dough for 8 minutes. Stop mixer.

4. Transfer dough to clean counter and knead dough for 30 seconds, then form dough into smooth ball (see photos, page 61).

5. Spray large bowl with vegetable oil spray. Place dough in greased bowl and cover with plastic wrap. Let dough rise until doubled in size, 1½ to 2 hours.

6. Transfer dough to clean counter and use your hands to gently press down on dough to pop any large bubbles. Pat dough into 6-inch square and use bench scraper to cut dough into 9 equal squares (following photos, page 70). Form each piece of dough into tight, smooth ball.

KEEP GOING!

YOU SAY "BALL," I SAY "BOULE"

The fancy French word for dough shaped in a ball is *boule*. Bread makers use the same technique (see photos, pages 61 and 70) to form a tight ball of dough for a large loaf of bread and for small individual dough balls such as these fluffy dinner rolls. While it takes two hands to form a large loaf into a boule, you can make a small one with just one cupped hand. If you get really good at it, you can even do two balls at once—one in each hand!

7. Spray inside bottom and sides of 8-inch square metal baking pan with vegetable oil spray. Arrange dough balls in 3 rows in greased baking pan. Cover baking pan loosely with plastic. Let dough balls rise until doubled in size, about 1 hour.

8. While dough rises, adjust oven rack to middle position and heat oven to 350 degrees.

9. When dough is ready, use pastry brush to paint tops of dough balls with beaten egg.

10. Place baking pan in oven. Bake until rolls are golden brown, 20 to 25 minutes.

11. Use oven mitts to remove baking pan from oven (ask an adult for help). Place baking pan on cooling rack and let rolls cool in pan for 30 minutes. Turn baking pan upside down to release rolls from pan. Turn rolls right side up and use your hands to pull them apart. Serve warm or at room temperature.

SHAPING FLUFFY DINNER ROLLS

Use your hands to create cute little dough balls—the perfect size for dinner rolls!

1. Pat dough into 6-inch square. Use bench scraper to cut square into 3 equal strips, then cut each strip into 3 equal pieces (you should have 9 pieces of dough).

2. Working with 1 piece of dough at a time, on clean counter, fold corners of dough into center and pinch edges together. Flip dough over.

3. Use your cupped hand to drag ball in small circles until top feels tight. Repeat with remaining pieces of dough.

CINNAMON ROLLS

MAKES 8 ROLLS
TOTAL TIME: 1 HOUR AND 35 MINUTES,
PLUS 1½ HOURS RISING TIME,
PLUS 15 MINUTES COOLING TIME

PREPARE INGREDIENTS

Dough
2¼ cups (11¼ ounces) all-purpose
   flour, plus extra for counter
3 tablespoons sugar
1½ teaspoons instant or rapid-rise
   yeast
¾ teaspoon salt
½ cup (4 ounces) room-temperature
   water
4 tablespoons unsalted butter,
   cut into 4 pieces and softened (see
   page 13 for how to soften butter)
1 large egg
Vegetable oil spray

Filling
¾ cup packed (5¼ ounces) light
   brown sugar
1¼ teaspoons ground cinnamon
⅛ teaspoon salt
2 tablespoons unsalted butter
Glaze (optional)

GATHER BAKING EQUIPMENT

Stand mixer with dough hook attachment
Whisk
Rubber spatula
3 bowls (1 large, 1 medium,
   1 small microwave-safe)
Plastic wrap
9-inch round metal cake pan
9-inch round piece of parchment paper
   (see page 146)
Ruler
Pastry brush
Bench scraper (or kitchen shears)
Oven mitts
Cooling rack
Butter knife

> "We had to wait so long, but they were
> worth the wait. They tasted delicious.
> I even licked the extra frosting."
> —Sonia, 9

1. **For the dough:** In bowl of stand mixer, whisk together flour, sugar, yeast, and salt. Lock bowl in place and attach dough hook to stand mixer.

2. Add water, 4 tablespoons softened butter, and egg to flour mixture. Start mixer on low speed and mix until no dry flour remains, about 2 minutes. Increase speed to medium and knead dough for 8 minutes. Stop mixer.

3. Sprinkle extra flour on clean counter and coat your hands with extra flour. Use rubber spatula to scrape dough onto floured counter and use your floured hands to knead dough for 30 seconds (see photos, page 61). Move dough to clean portion of counter and use your hands to form dough into smooth ball.

4. Spray inside of large bowl with vegetable oil spray. Place dough in greased bowl and cover bowl with plastic wrap. Let dough rise until doubled in size, 1 to 1½ hours.

5. While dough rises, spray inside bottom and sides of 9-inch round metal cake pan with vegetable oil spray. Line bottom of cake pan with 9-inch parchment paper round.

KEEP GOING! →

EASIER ROLLING

Traditionally, when making cinnamon rolls, you slather softened butter and sprinkle cinnamon sugar all over a big rectangle of yeasted dough and then roll it up into a long, tight log. Then, you cut the log into pieces to get individual rolls. We found that it was pretty tricky to roll up a giant rectangle of dough. Instead, we cut individual strips of buttered and cinnamon-sugared dough and rolled them up one at a time—so much easier!

⌇⌇⌇ GLAZE ⌇⌇⌇ IT UP! ⌇⌇

If you want to make your rolls just a little more special, add a glaze!

To make glaze: In small bowl, whisk together ½ cup (2 ounces) confectioners' (powdered) sugar and 2 teaspoons milk. (Glaze should be thin enough to drizzle from end of spoon. Add up to 1 teaspoon additional milk as needed to adjust consistency.)

Use spoon to drizzle glaze over warm rolls.

6. **For the filling:** In medium bowl, use clean rubber spatula to stir together brown sugar, cinnamon, and salt.

7. When dough is ready, melt 2 tablespoons butter in small microwave-safe bowl (see page 13 for how to melt butter). Transfer dough to clean counter and shape, fill, and roll up rolls (following photos, right).

8. Use bench scraper (or your hands) to scoop up any filling left on counter and sprinkle it evenly over rolls. Spray sheet of plastic wrap with vegetable oil spray. Cover cake pan loosely with greased plastic and let rolls rise at room temperature until puffy, 30 to 45 minutes.

9. While rolls rise, adjust oven rack to middle position and heat oven to 325 degrees.

10. When rolls are ready, discard plastic from cake pan. Place cake pan in oven. Bake until rolls are golden brown, 40 to 45 minutes.

11. Use oven mitts to remove cake pan from oven (ask an adult for help). Place cake pan on cooling rack and let rolls cool in pan for 15 minutes. Run butter knife around edge of cake pan to release rolls from pan. Drizzle with glaze, if using (see Glaze It Up!, left). Serve warm or at room temperature.

SHAPING CINNAMON ROLLS

1. Pat dough into 16-by-8-inch rectangle with long side parallel to counter's edge. Use pastry brush to paint melted butter evenly over dough. Sprinkle filling evenly over dough, leaving 1-inch border at top.

2. Use bench scraper to cut dough into eight 2-inch-wide strips.

3. Roll each strip away from you into tight log.

4. Place roll, spiral side up, in parchment paper–lined cake pan. Arrange 7 rolls around outside of cake pan and place 1 roll in center.

SOFT PRETZELS

MAKES 6 PRETZELS
**TOTAL TIME: 1¼ HOURS, PLUS 1 HOUR RISING TIME,
PLUS 10 MINUTES COOLING TIME**

PREPARE INGREDIENTS

Dough
2 cups (11 ounces) bread flour
1 teaspoon instant or rapid-rise yeast
2 teaspoons kosher salt
1 tablespoon vegetable oil
1 tablespoon packed brown sugar
¾ cup (6 ounces) room-temperature water
Vegetable oil spray

To Finish and Bake
1 tablespoon baking soda
½ cup (4 ounces) water
1 teaspoon pretzel salt (or kosher salt)
3 tablespoons unsalted butter

GATHER BAKING EQUIPMENT

Stand mixer with dough hook attachment
Whisk
4-cup liquid measuring cup
2 bowls (1 large, 1 small microwave-safe)
Plastic wrap
Rimmed baking sheet
Aluminum foil

2 cooling racks
Oven mitts
Spoon
Ruler
Bench scraper (or kitchen shears)
Pastry brush

"Ranch would probably be really good with it!"
—Zachary, 13

"Soft, crunchy, salty. 10/10." —Max, 11

1. **For the dough:** In bowl of stand mixer, whisk together flour, yeast, and 2 teaspoons kosher salt. Lock bowl into place and attach dough hook to stand mixer.

2. In 4-cup liquid measuring cup, whisk together oil, brown sugar, and ¾ cup water until brown sugar has dissolved.

3. Start mixer on low speed and slowly pour in water mixture. Mix until no dry flour is visible, about 2 minutes. Increase speed to medium and knead dough for 8 minutes. Stop mixer.

4. Transfer dough to clean counter and use your hands to knead dough for 30 seconds, then form dough into smooth ball (see photos, page 61).

5. Spray inside of large bowl with vegetable oil spray. Place dough in greased bowl. Cover bowl with plastic wrap and let dough rise until doubled in size, 1 to 1½ hours.

KEEP GOING! ⟫⟫⟶

BOILING OVER

One of the weirdest (and coolest) things about traditional pretzels (and bagels) is that they are boiled in water before they're baked. Bakers drop the shaped breads into a boiling water bath for just a minute or two to help set the crust on the outside and make them extra chewy inside. The water sometimes also has a chemical called lye in it, which gives the crust a dark brown color and tangy flavor. Since boiling pretzels at home can be tricky (and dangerous), we skip that step and still get a nice brown crust by painting them all over with baking soda dissolved in water. These pretzels bake up beautifully—no boiling water required!

THE MAGIC OF YEAST

Yeast is a single-celled living organism. It's actually a microscopic fungus! You buy yeast in small packets at the grocery store. The yeast is "sleeping." Mixing the yeast with a liquid (usually water) wakes up the yeast so it can turn flour into bread dough. So how exactly does that work?

Yeast feeds on the starches in the flour and produces carbon dioxide in the process. Carbon dioxide causes the dough to rise, much like blowing air into chewing gum to make a bubble. All those tiny holes inside a loaf of chewy rustic bread? That's the handiwork of the yeast.

All our bread recipes use instant yeast (sometimes labeled rapid-rise yeast), because it is the most reliable option for home bakers. Keep yeast in the refrigerator and check the package dates—old yeast won't work. Do not use active dry yeast in these recipes.

6. **To finish and bake:** While dough rises, adjust oven rack to middle position and heat oven to 425 degrees. Line rimmed baking sheet with aluminum foil. Set 1 cooling rack in baking sheet and spray well with vegetable oil spray.

7. Combine baking soda and remaining ½ cup water in small microwave-safe bowl. Heat in microwave until water looks clear, 1 to 2 minutes. Use oven mitts to remove bowl from microwave (be careful—bowl will be hot). Use spoon to stir mixture until baking soda has completely dissolved. Set aside to cool.

8. When dough is ready, transfer dough to clean counter. Gently press and stretch dough into 6-inch square, popping any large bubbles. Use bench scraper to cut dough into 6 equal 1-inch-wide strips. Cover dough strips loosely with plastic.

9. Use your hands to stretch and roll 1 piece of dough into 22-inch-long rope (keep remaining pieces covered), then shape into pretzel (following photos, right). Place pretzel on greased cooling rack in baking sheet. Repeat with remaining dough strips, spacing pretzels about 2 inches apart on rack.

10. Use pastry brush to paint tops and sides of each pretzel with water–baking soda mixture (coat pretzels well for even browning, then discard extra mixture). Sprinkle tops of pretzels with 1 teaspoon pretzel salt.

11. Place baking sheet in oven. Bake until pretzels are deep golden brown, 10 to 12 minutes.

12. Use oven mitts to remove baking sheet from oven (ask an adult for help). Place baking sheet on second cooling rack and let pretzels cool on baking sheet for 10 minutes.

13. While pretzels cool, melt butter (see page 13 for how to melt butter). Use clean pastry brush to paint pretzels all over with melted butter. Serve warm.

SHAPING PRETZELS

Pretzels may look complicated, but follow these easy steps to create your own! Remember: even if they're not perfect, they will be delicious.

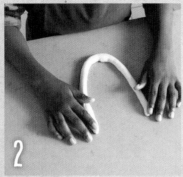

1. Use your hands to stretch and roll 1 piece of dough into 22-inch-long rope.

2. Shape rope into U, with curve at bottom and ends facing away from you.

3. Hold ends of ropes and twist twice near top of U.

4. Fold ends over toward bottom of U.

5. Press ends into bottom of U, spaced about 1 inch apart.

CHAPTER 3: PIZZA, FLATBREAD & OTHER SAVORY BAKED GOODS

FROM PERSONAL PIZZAS TO BEEF EMPANADAS, BAKING ISN'T ALWAYS ABOUT THE SWEET!

PIZZA DOUGH

MAKES ABOUT 1 POUND
TOTAL TIME: 30 MINUTES,
**   PLUS 1 HOUR RISING TIME**

PREPARE INGREDIENTS

Vegetable oil spray
¾ cup (6 ounces) ice water (see page 11
    for how to measure ice water)
1 tablespoon extra-virgin olive oil
1⅔ cups (9⅛ ounces) bread flour
1 teaspoon instant or rapid-rise yeast
1 teaspoon sugar
1 teaspoon salt

GATHER BAKING EQUIPMENT

Large bowl
Liquid measuring cup
Food processor
Plastic wrap

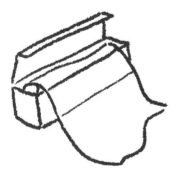

IT'S A PIZZA DOUGH SLEEPOVER!

Pizza dough needs time to rise. The yeast creates little bubbles of carbon dioxide—plus a lot of flavor. But you don't have to make your dough and your pizza on the same day. You can let your dough rise in the refrigerator overnight. The cold temperature of the fridge slows down the yeast's activity. The dough will still rise, but it will rise more slowly.

After putting the dough in the bowl and covering the bowl in step 6, transfer it to the refrigerator and let it rise there for up to 24 hours. When you're ready to use the dough, you'll need to warm it back up to room temperature. You can either leave the bowl out on the counter for 1 to 2 hours or use our hot water trick: Place the cold dough in a zipper-lock plastic bag, squeeze out the extra air, and seal the bag. Place the bag in a large bowl filled with hot water. Turn and squeeze the dough a few times until it's warmed all the way through, about 15 minutes.

1. Spray inside bottom and sides of large bowl with vegetable oil spray and set aside. In liquid measuring cup, combine water and oil.

2. Add flour, yeast, and sugar to food processor and lock lid into place. Hold down pulse button for 1 second, then release. Repeat until ingredients are combined, about five 1-second pulses.

3. Turn on processor, then slowly pour water mixture through feed tube and process until dough comes together and no dry flour remains, about 30 seconds. Stop processor. Let dough sit for 10 minutes.

4. Remove processor lid and sprinkle salt over dough. Lock lid back into place. Turn on processor and process for 1 minute. Stop processor.

5. Remove lid and carefully remove processor blade (ask an adult for help). Lightly spray counter and your hands with vegetable oil spray. Transfer dough to greased counter and use your greased hands to knead dough for 30 seconds, then form dough into smooth ball (see photos, page 61).

6. Place dough in greased bowl and cover with plastic wrap. Let dough rise until bubbly and doubled in size, 1 to 1½ hours. Use dough to make Personal Pizzas (page 84) or Tear-and-Share Pepperoni Pizza Rolls (page 88).

PERSONAL PIZZAS

MAKES 4 (7-INCH) PIZZAS
TOTAL TIME: 1 HOUR AND 10 MINUTES
   (PLUS TIME TO MAKE PIZZA DOUGH,
   IF MAKING)

PREPARE INGREDIENTS

Vegetable oil spray
1 pound pizza dough, room temperature
   (see page 82 to make your own, or use
   store-bought)
All-purpose flour (for sprinkling on counter)
½ cup pizza sauce (see page 87 to make
   your own, or use store-bought)
1 cup shredded mozzarella cheese
   (4 ounces)
¼ cup grated Parmesan cheese (½ ounce)

GATHER BAKING EQUIPMENT

2 rimmed baking sheets
Bench scraper (or kitchen scissors or knife)
Ruler
Plastic wrap
Rolling pin
1-tablespoon measuring spoon
¼-cup dry measuring cup
Oven mitts
Cooling rack
Spatula
Cutting board
Pizza wheel or chef's knife

"Loved the quick and easy sauce.
Delicious. Perfect crust. I would add
a little more sauce." —Helen, 12

"The dough was tricky but really yummy.
Sauce was amazing!" —Claire, 10

1. Adjust oven rack to lowest position and heat oven to 450 degrees. Spray 2 rimmed baking sheets well with vegetable oil spray.

2. Place room-temperature dough on clean counter. Use bench scraper to divide dough into 4 equal pieces. Pat each piece of dough into 3½-inch circle.

3. Spray piece of plastic wrap lightly with vegetable oil spray. Cover dough pieces with greased plastic. Let rise on counter until slightly puffy, about 15 minutes. (This is a good time to make your sauce!)

4. Sprinkle clean counter lightly with flour. Remove one piece of dough from under plastic and place on lightly floured counter. Flip dough over to coat with flour. Use rolling pin to roll into 7-inch circle, rotating dough in between rolls (following photos, below).

KEEP GOING! ⟫⟫⟫→

↻ ↻ ROLLING PERSONAL PIZZAS ↻ ↻

1. Sprinkle clean counter lightly with flour. Remove 1 piece of dough from under plastic and place on lightly floured counter. Flip dough over to coat with flour. Use rolling pin to roll dough, starting in center.

2. Rotate dough clockwise in between rolls to create even circle and to make sure dough does not stick to counter.

3. Continue to roll into 7-inch circle. (If dough snaps back when you roll it out, cover it with greased plastic and let it rest for 10 minutes, then try again.)

5. Transfer rolled dough to one greased baking sheet. Repeat rolling with one more piece of dough and place on same baking sheet.

6. Spoon 1 to 2 tablespoons sauce into center of each pizza and use back of spoon to spread into even layer, leaving ¼-inch border around edge.

7. Sprinkle each pizza with ¼ cup mozzarella cheese and 1 tablespoon Parmesan cheese. Top with your favorite toppings (see Make It Your Way, right).

8. Place baking sheet in oven and bake pizzas until edges are browned and cheeses are well browned and bubbling, 10 to 12 minutes.

9. While first 2 pizzas are baking, shape and top 2 more pizzas, repeating steps 4 through 7 with remaining 2 dough balls, sauce, cheeses, and toppings. Place pizzas on second greased baking sheet.

10. Use oven mitts to remove first baking sheet from oven (ask an adult for help). Place baking sheet on cooling rack and let pizzas cool for 5 minutes. While first 2 pizzas are cooling, bake second batch of pizzas until edges are browned and cheeses are well browned and bubbling, 10 to 12 minutes.

11. Use spatula to loosen edges of cooled pizzas from baking sheets, then carefully transfer to cutting board (baking sheets will be hot). Use pizza wheel or chef's knife to slice pizzas and serve.

ALL ABOUT THE CRUST

There are so many kinds of pizzas in the world. Thick, thin, deep dish, slab, square, and beyond. Here, we're creating personal pizzas with crispy crusts. To become crispy, the crust needs to bake quickly and therefore needs as much heat as possible. The oven's heat source is usually on the bottom of the oven, so we try to get the baking sheet as close to it as possible! That's why we bake 2 pizzas on one baking sheet at a time.

EASY PIZZA SAUCE

MAKES 1 CUP
TOTAL TIME: 15 MINUTES

PREPARE INGREDIENTS

1 (14.5-ounce) can whole peeled
   tomatoes, opened
1 tablespoon extra-virgin olive oil
1 garlic clove, peeled
½ teaspoon red wine vinegar
½ teaspoon dried oregano
¼ teaspoon salt
⅛ teaspoon pepper

GATHER COOKING EQUIPMENT

Colander
Food processor
Rubber spatula
Medium bowl

START BAKING! ←‒‒‒‒

1. Set colander in sink. Pour tomatoes into colander. Shake colander to drain tomatoes well.

2. Transfer drained tomatoes to food processor. Add oil, garlic, vinegar, oregano, salt, and pepper. Lock lid into place. Turn on processor and process mixture until smooth, about 30 seconds. Stop processor.

3. Remove lid and carefully remove processor blade (ask an adult for help). Use rubber spatula to transfer sauce to medium bowl. (Sauce can be covered and refrigerated for up to 2 days.)

MAKE IT YOUR WAY

Add some toppings to your pizza to make it just the way you want it. But keep this in mind: less is more. Adding too many toppings (especially if they are heavy or wet) will make your pizza soggy and steamy instead of crunchy and crispy. Scatter a few toppings evenly over the pizza, making sure you can still see the cheese in between them, and you'll be good to go.

ADD THESE TOPPINGS BEFORE BAKING
Pepperoni slices, cooked **sausage**, cooked **bacon**, cooked **chicken**, quartered **cherry tomatoes**, sliced **bell peppers**, sliced **mushrooms**, pitted **olives**, crumbled **feta** or **goat cheese**, fresh **mozzarella balls.**

ADD THESE TOPPINGS AFTER BAKING
Torn fresh **basil** leaves, a handful of **baby arugula** or **baby spinach**, small spoonfuls of **pesto**, small spoonfuls of **ricotta cheese**, extra grated **Parmesan cheese**, crushed **red pepper flakes.**

TEAR-AND-SHARE PEPPERONI PIZZA ROLLS

MAKES 12 ROLLS
TOTAL TIME: 1¾ HOURS, PLUS 45 MINUTES
TO 1 HOUR RISING TIME,
PLUS 25 MINUTES COOLING TIME
(PLUS TIME TO MAKE PIZZA DOUGH,
IF MAKING)

PREPARE INGREDIENTS

Vegetable oil spray
1 pound pizza dough, room temperature
   (see page 82 to make your own, or use
   store-bought)
24 slices pepperoni
1 cup shredded mozzarella cheese
   (4 ounces)
1 tablespoon extra-virgin olive oil
1 garlic clove, minced
¼ cup grated Parmesan cheese (½ ounce)
1 cup pizza sauce, warmed (see page 87
   to make your own, or use store-bought)

GATHER BAKING EQUIPMENT

8-inch round piece of parchment paper (see page 146)
8-inch round metal cake pan
Ruler
Bench scraper (or kitchen shears)
Plastic wrap
1-tablespoon measuring spoon
Small microwave-safe bowl
Pastry brush
Oven mitts
Cooling rack
Butter knife

1. Adjust oven rack to lowest position and heat oven to 400 degrees. Place parchment paper round in bottom of 8-inch round metal cake pan. Spray inside bottom and sides of pan lightly with vegetable oil spray.

2. Spray clean counter lightly with vegetable oil spray. Transfer room-temperature dough to greased counter. Gently press and stretch dough into 6-inch square, popping any large bubbles. Use bench scraper to cut square into 12 equal pieces (see photo, below). Cover dough pieces with plastic wrap.

3. Remove 1 piece of dough from under plastic (keep remaining pieces covered). Shape, fill, and form 1 roll with pepperoni and mozzarella cheese (following photos, below). Flip dough ball over and place in parchment-lined cake pan. Repeat with remaining dough pieces, pepperoni, and mozzarella cheese.

KEEP GOING! ≫≫→

SHAPING TEAR-AND-SHARE PIZZA ROLLS

The slices of pepperoni help seal the cheese inside each roll. You can substitute vegetarian pepperoni if you prefer, but don't omit the pepperoni!

1. Gently press and stretch dough into 6-inch square. Use bench scraper to cut square into 4 equal strips. Cut each strip into 3 equal pieces (you'll have 12 pieces total).

2. Pat 1 piece of dough into 3-inch circle. Place 1 slice pepperoni in center of circle. Top pepperoni with heaping 1 tablespoon shredded mozzarella cheese and second slice pepperoni.

3. Fold edges of dough up and over filling and pinch edges well to close. Flip ball over and place in parchment-lined cake pan.

4. Cover cake pan with plastic and let rise until dough balls are slightly puffed and touching each other, 45 minutes to 1 hour.

5. Meanwhile, in small microwave-safe bowl, combine oil and garlic. Heat in microwave until warm and garlic is fragrant, 15 to 30 seconds.

6. Once dough has risen, remove plastic. Use pastry brush to paint tops of dough balls with garlic oil. Sprinkle evenly with Parmesan cheese.

7. Place cake pan in oven and bake until tops of rolls are well browned, 30 to 35 minutes.

8. Use oven mitts to remove cake pan from oven (ask an adult for help). Place pan on cooling rack and let rolls cool in pan for 15 minutes.

9. Carefully run butter knife around edge of cake pan to loosen rolls from pan (pan will be hot). Use oven mitts to carefully turn pan on its side and remove rolls from pan. Let rolls cool directly on cooling rack for 10 minutes. (This is a great time to warm up your pizza sauce.) Serve with warm pizza sauce for dipping.

THE BEST SNACK...EVER?

Pizza is tasty. "Tear-and-share" bread (often called monkey bread) is delicious. But combining the two? Out of this world. We took the flavors of pizza (melty mozzarella cheese, pepperoni, pizza dough) and combined them with the structure of tear-and-share bread (knotty-looking balls of dough that are served warm and pulled apart with your hands) for the ultimate snack. Just don't forget the pizza sauce for dipping!

BUFFALO CHICKEN LAVASH FLATBREAD

SERVES 2 TO 4
TOTAL TIME: 45 MINUTES

PREPARE INGREDIENTS

1 (12-by-9-inch) lavash bread
1 tablespoon extra-virgin olive oil
1 cup shredded cooked chicken (from
   rotisserie chicken or from leftovers)
2 tablespoons Frank's hot sauce (or
   other not-too-spicy hot sauce)
1 tablespoon unsalted butter, melted
   (see page 13 for how to melt butter)
¾ cup shredded Monterey Jack cheese
   (3 ounces)
½ cup baby spinach, chopped
Ranch dressing (optional)

GATHER BAKING EQUIPMENT

Rimmed baking sheet
Pastry brush
Oven mitts
Cooling rack
Medium bowl
Rubber spatula
Spatula
Cutting board
Chef's knife

"The hot sauce provided just the right amount of zing to the chicken." —John, 10

"If you double the recipe, don't double the hot sauce (we used Tapatio Picante). It was a little too spicy, so you could barely taste the cheese." —Keegan, 9

1. Adjust oven rack to lower-middle position and heat oven to 425 degrees. Lay lavash on rimmed baking sheet. Use pastry brush to paint both sides of lavash evenly with oil.

2. Place baking sheet in oven and bake until lavash is light golden brown, 3 to 4 minutes.

3. Use oven mitts to remove baking sheet from oven (ask an adult for help). Place baking sheet on cooling rack. Let lavash cool on baking sheet for 10 minutes.

4. While lavash is cooling, in medium bowl, combine chicken, hot sauce, and melted butter. Use rubber spatula to stir until chicken is well coated with sauce.

5. Sprinkle cheese evenly over cooled lavash. Spread chicken mixture evenly over cheese. Sprinkle with spinach.

6. Use oven mitts to return baking sheet to oven and bake until cheese is melted and chicken is warmed through, 4 to 6 minutes.

7. Use oven mitts to remove baking sheet from oven (ask an adult for help). Place baking sheet on cooling rack. Let lavash cool slightly on baking sheet, about 2 minutes. Use spatula to transfer lavash to cutting board (ask an adult for help—baking sheet will be hot). Cut into pieces and serve with ranch dressing, if using.

WHAT IS BUFFALO SAUCE?

Invented in the city of Buffalo, New York, in the 1960s, Buffalo sauce is simply a combination of hot sauce and butter. It was first used to coat deep-fried chicken wings, a popular late-night restaurant snack. Today you can find all kinds of Buffalo-flavored items on menus and in stores—wings, pizzas, chips, crackers, and even soda! The key to Buffalo sauce is the kind of hot sauce you use—it should be slightly thick, vinegary, and not too hot (Tabasco and sriracha are too spicy). The classic brand used in the original recipe is Frank's Red Hot Original Cayenne Pepper Sauce, which is tangy, a bit sweet, and spicy without being overpowering.

CORN, TOMATO, AND BACON GALETTE

SERVES 6
TOTAL TIME: 1½ HOURS,
    PLUS 15 MINUTES COOLING TIME
    (PLUS TIME TO MAKE PIE DOUGH, IF MAKING)

PREPARE INGREDIENTS

All-purpose flour (for sprinkling on counter)
1 recipe Pie Dough (see page 194 to make
    your own, or use 1 round store-bought)
3 slices bacon
1 cup frozen corn, thawed and patted dry
1 cup (6 ounces) cherry tomatoes, halved
½ cup shredded cheddar cheese (2 ounces)
1 garlic clove, peeled and minced
¼ teaspoon salt
¼ cup grated Parmesan cheese (½ ounce)
1 large egg, cracked into bowl and lightly
    beaten with fork (see page 14)
1 scallion, dark green part only, sliced thin

GATHER BAKING EQUIPMENT

Rimmed baking sheet
Parchment paper
Rolling pin
Ruler
Plastic wrap
Microwave-safe plate
Paper towels
Oven mitts
Large bowl
Rubber spatula
Pastry brush
Cooling rack
Large spatula
Cutting board
Chef's knife

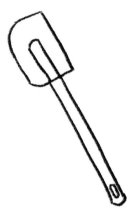

START BAKING! ←《《《《《

1. Adjust oven rack to lower-middle position and heat oven to 375 degrees. Line rimmed baking sheet with parchment paper.

2. If using homemade Pie Dough (page 194), sprinkle flour over clean counter. Place dough on floured counter and sprinkle dough with a little extra flour. Use rolling pin to roll dough into 12-inch circle, rotating dough and reflouring counter in between rolls (see photos, page 196). (Store-bought dough is already rolled out.)

3. Use your hands to gently transfer dough to parchment-lined baking sheet. Cover baking sheet loosely with plastic wrap and refrigerate while making filling.

4. Line microwave-safe plate with 2 paper towels and place bacon on top. Top with 2 more paper towels. Cook in microwave until bacon is crispy, 3 to 5 minutes. Use oven mitts to remove plate from microwave—plate will be hot. Let bacon cool.

5. In large bowl, use rubber spatula to stir together corn, tomatoes, cheddar cheese, garlic, and salt.

6. Remove baking sheet from refrigerator and discard plastic. Sprinkle Parmesan cheese evenly over dough, leaving 2-inch border around edge. Use rubber spatula to spread corn-tomato mixture over Parmesan. Use your hands to crumble cooked bacon over top.

7. Fold 2-inch border of dough up and over edge of filling (see photos, page 203). Continue folding, overlapping folds of dough every 2 inches, until you get all the way around galette. Use pastry brush to paint dough with beaten egg.

8. Place baking sheet in oven and bake until dough is golden brown, 45 to 50 minutes.

9. Use oven mitts to remove baking sheet from oven (ask an adult for help). Place baking sheet on cooling rack. Let galette cool on baking sheet for 15 minutes. Use large spatula to transfer galette to cutting board. Sprinkle scallion greens over filling. Slice into wedges and serve warm or at room temperature.

SOGGY CRUST SAVER

A galette is like a pie, except the crust is only on the bottom and the sides, and it's totally free-form (no pie plate here!). A good galette has a crust that is nice and crisp. But the filling can create a problem. Most veggies are filled with water, which can make the crust wet. The solution? We put a layer of grated Parmesan cheese on the bottom of the galette before adding the filling. This creates a (delicious!) barrier against any excess water. It's also important to bake the galette right after assembling it. Don't let it sit around and get soggy!

MINI BEEF AND CHEESE EMPANADAS

MAKES 10 EMPANADAS
TOTAL TIME: 1¾ HOURS,
   PLUS 15 MINUTES COOLING TIME (PLUS TIME
   TO MAKE PIE DOUGH, IF MAKING)

PREPARE INGREDIENTS

All-purpose flour (for sprinkling on counter)
1 recipe Pie Dough (see page 194 to make
   your own, or use 2 rounds store-bought)
1 teaspoon plus 1 tablespoon extra-virgin
   olive oil, measured separately
6 ounces 85-percent lean ground beef
1 shallot, peeled and minced
1 tablespoon tomato paste
2 garlic cloves, peeled and minced
½ teaspoon ground cumin
¼ teaspoon salt
¼ cup (2 ounces) water, plus extra for
   shaping empanadas
½ cup shredded Monterey Jack cheese
   (2 ounces)
1 tablespoon minced fresh cilantro (see
   page 17 for how to mince herbs)

GATHER BAKING EQUIPMENT

Rimmed baking sheet
Parchment paper
Rolling pin
Ruler
3¾-inch round biscuit cutter (or drinking glass with
   same diameter)
Plastic wrap
10-inch nonstick skillet
Wooden spoon
Medium bowl
1-tablespoon measuring spoon
Fork
Pastry brush
Oven mitts
Cooling rack

START BAKING!

1. Adjust oven rack to middle position and heat oven to 425 degrees. Line rimmed baking sheet with parchment paper.

2. If using homemade Pie Dough (page 194), sprinkle flour over clean counter. Place dough on floured counter and sprinkle dough with a little extra flour. Use rolling pin to roll dough into 14-inch circle, about ⅛ inch thick, rotating dough and reflouring counter in between rolls (see photos, page 196). (Store-bought dough is already rolled out.)

3. Using 3¾-inch round biscuit cutter, cut out 10 rounds of dough, discarding dough scraps. Transfer dough rounds to parchment-lined baking sheet. Cover baking sheet loosely with plastic and refrigerate while making filling.

4. In 10-inch nonstick skillet, heat 1 teaspoon oil over medium heat for 1 minute (oil should be hot but not smoking). Add beef, shallot, tomato paste, garlic, cumin, and salt. Cook until beef is no longer pink, about 3 minutes, stirring often with wooden spoon to break up meat.

KEEP GOING! ⟫⟫⟶

 **MAKE IT YOUR WAY**

You can stuff these savory pockets with just about anything! We made a classic ground beef and cheese filling, but you can also try our vegetarian option with black beans. But don't stop there. You can get creative, making empanada fillings out of different kinds of cooked meats, vegetables, and cheeses. Just be sure to follow our sealing and crimping directions so the good stuff doesn't burst out of the dough wrappers.

MINI BEAN AND CHEESE EMPANADAS

Use 1 cup rinsed **black beans** instead of ground beef and ½ cup **shredded sharp cheddar cheese** instead of Monterey Jack cheese. In step 4, add beans along with shallot and cook until warmed through, about 3 minutes. In step 5, use back of wooden spoon to mash up beans in bowl before refrigerating.

5. Carefully pour ¼ cup water into skillet and cook until mixture is thick but not dry, 1 to 2 minutes. Transfer mixture to medium bowl and let cool slightly, then refrigerate mixture until completely cooled, about 30 minutes.

6. Once filling is chilled, use clean wooden spoon to stir in cheese and cilantro.

7. Remove baking sheet from refrigerator and discard plastic. Use 1-tablespoon measuring spoon to place 1 tablespoon filling in center of each dough round. Shape, seal, and crimp empanadas (following photos, below).

8. Use pastry brush to paint tops and sides of empanadas with remaining 1 tablespoon oil. Place baking sheet in oven and bake until empanadas are golden brown, 18 to 22 minutes.

9. Use oven mitts to remove baking sheet from oven (ask an adult for help). Place baking sheet on cooling rack and let empanadas cool on baking sheet for at least 15 minutes. Serve.

  # SHAPING EMPANADAS

If using store-bought pie dough in place of our homemade dough for this recipe, you will need one package (containing two pie rounds) to get 10 empanadas. Reduce the baking time by 2 minutes.

1. Dip your finger in water and lightly moisten edges of each dough round.

2. Fold dough over filling to create half-moon shape. Use your fingers to press edges together to seal.

3. Use fork to press sealed edges together to crimp dough.

"It had a nice texture. The outside was crisp and the inside was gooey." —Gillian, 13

BRAZILIAN CHEESE BREAD (PÃO DE QUEIJO)

MAKES 12 ROLLS
TOTAL TIME: 1 HOUR, PLUS 5 MINUTES
    COOLING TIME

PREPARE INGREDIENTS

Vegetable oil spray
1 cup (8 ounces) whole milk
1 cup shredded extra-sharp cheddar cheese
    (4 ounces)
1 cup grated Pecorino Romano cheese
    (2 ounces)
⅓ cup extra-virgin olive oil
2 large eggs
1 teaspoon salt
2 cups (8 ounces) tapioca starch

GATHER BAKING EQUIPMENT

12-cup muffin tin
Blender
Dish towel
Rubber spatula
Oven mitts
Cooling rack
Butter knife

THE SECRET OF THESE STRETCHY, CHEWY BITES

Brazilian cheese bread rolls (*pão de queijo*) are small rolls with crunchy exteriors and uniquely chewy, stretchy centers. Instead of using flour like most baked goods, they use a surprise ingredient: tapioca starch. Tapioca starch (also called tapioca flour) is made from cassava root (a plant native to South America) that has been ground up into a powder. When combined with liquid, tapioca starch makes a gooey paste that can trap air and make baked goods rise in the oven. Bonus: it's naturally gluten-free!

CHAPTER 3:

1. Adjust oven rack to middle position and heat oven to 375 degrees. Spray 12-cup muffin tin with vegetable oil spray (making sure to get inside each cup).

2. Add milk, cheddar cheese, Pecorino cheese, oil, eggs, and salt to blender. Add tapioca starch. (Make sure to add the tapioca starch last, or the mixture will turn to glue in the blender.) Place lid on top of blender and hold lid firmly in place with folded dish towel (see Blender Safety, right). Process on high speed for 30 seconds. Stop blender.

3. Use rubber spatula to scrape down sides of blender jar. Replace lid and process on high speed until smooth, about 30 seconds. Pour batter evenly into greased muffin tin cups, filling each cup about three-quarters full.

4. Place muffin tin in oven and bake until rolls are golden and puffed, 25 to 30 minutes.

5. Use oven mitts to remove muffin tin from oven (ask an adult for help). Place muffin tin on cooling rack and let rolls cool in muffin tin for 5 minutes.

6. Run butter knife around edges of rolls to loosen from muffin tin (ask an adult for help—muffin tin will be very hot). Using your fingertips, gently wiggle rolls to remove from muffin tin and transfer directly to cooling rack. Serve warm.

BLENDER SAFETY

When using the blender to process a batter, make a smoothie, or puree a soup, follow two simple rules:

- Don't fill the blender jar more than two-thirds full.
- Make sure to hold the lid securely in place with a folded dish towel.

Once ingredients are in the blender jar, place the lid on top and hold it firmly in place with a folded dish towel. Then turn on the blender, keeping pressure on the towel so the lid stays in place.

CHAPTER 4: COOKIES & BARS

COOKIES AND BARS CAN BE CHEWY, CRISPY, OR CRUNCHY, SQUARE OR ROUND, TALL OR SHORT. THE GOOD NEWS? ALL ARE TASTY.

OATMEAL-CHOCOLATE CHIP COOKIES

MAKES 12 COOKIES
TOTAL TIME: 40 MINUTES,
 PLUS 25 MINUTES COOLING TIME

PREPARE INGREDIENTS

½ cup (2½ ounces) all-purpose flour
½ teaspoon salt
¼ teaspoon baking soda
½ cup packed (3½ ounces) light brown
 sugar
¼ cup vegetable oil
2 tablespoons unsalted butter,
 melted and cooled (see page 13
 for how to melt butter)
⅛ teaspoon ground cinnamon
1 large egg
½ teaspoon vanilla extract
1½ cups (4½ ounces) old-fashioned
 rolled oats (see right for more
 information on oats)
¼ cup (1½ ounces) chocolate chips

GATHER BAKING EQUIPMENT

Rimmed baking sheet
Parchment paper
2 bowls (1 large, 1 medium)
Whisk
Rubber spatula
1-tablespoon measuring spoon
Ruler
Oven mitts
Cooling rack
Spatula

> "It was super chewy (not in a bad way) and tasted best warm." —Elena, 12

> "This was a delicious cookie and I REALLY LOVED IT!" —Emma, 10

1. Adjust oven rack to middle position and heat oven to 375 degrees. Line rimmed baking sheet with parchment paper.

2. In medium bowl, whisk together flour, salt, and baking soda.

3. In large bowl, whisk together brown sugar, oil, melted butter, and cinnamon. Add egg and vanilla and whisk until mixture is smooth.

4. Add flour mixture to sugar mixture and use rubber spatula to stir until fully combined, about 1 minute. Add oats and chocolate chips and stir until evenly distributed.

5. Use 1-tablespoon measuring spoon to drop dough onto parchment-lined baking sheet in 12 mounds (about 2 heaping tablespoons each). Leave space between mounds (see photo, page 108). Wet your hand lightly, then use your damp hand to gently flatten each mound into 2-inch-wide circle.

6. Place baking sheet in oven. Bake cookies until edges are set and lightly browned but centers are still soft, 8 to 10 minutes.

7. Use oven mitts to remove baking sheet from oven (ask an adult for help). Place baking sheet on cooling rack and let cookies cool on baking sheet for 10 minutes.

8. Use spatula to transfer cookies directly to cooling rack and let cool completely, about 15 minutes. Serve.

OAT'S ABOUT TIME

Rolled oats (also called old-fashioned or regular oats) are whole oats that have been steamed and then rolled. If these same oats are rolled very thinly, they are called quick oats because they cook, well, more quickly. Instant oats are cooked and then dehydrated, so they don't need any more cooking, just hot water. Not all brands of rolled oats are the same—some are denser than others (they weigh more). For these cookies, we had the best luck using Quaker old-fashioned rolled oats. (We found that cookies made with Bob's Red Mill old-fashioned rolled oats spread out a bit more in the oven.) Don't use quick, instant, or extra-thick rolled oats in this recipe.

CHOCOLATE CRINKLE COOKIES

MAKES 12 COOKIES
TOTAL TIME: 50 MINUTES,
**   PLUS 30 MINUTES COOLING TIME**

PREPARE INGREDIENTS

½ cup (2½ ounces) all-purpose flour
¼ cup (¾ ounce) Dutch-processed cocoa
    powder
½ teaspoon baking powder
⅛ teaspoon baking soda
¼ teaspoon salt
¾ cup packed (5¼ ounces) brown sugar
1 large egg plus 1 large egg yolk
    (see page 14 for how to separate eggs)
½ teaspoon vanilla extract
2 ounces unsweetened chocolate
2 tablespoons unsalted butter
¼ cup (1¾ ounces) sugar
¼ cup (1 ounce) confectioners' (powdered)
    sugar

WHAT IS A CRINKLE COOKIE?

These deep, dark, chocolaty cookies are also known as "earthquakes" because of all the cracks that break through their snow-white surfaces during baking. The key to creating these crinkly cracks is rolling the formed dough first in granulated sugar and then in confectioners' sugar. The granulated sugar helps create that crackly, crusty exterior and keeps the confectioners' sugar coating in place so you can see the fissures.

GATHER BAKING EQUIPMENT

Rimmed baking sheet
Parchment paper
3 bowls (1 large, 1 medium,
    1 small microwave-safe)
Whisk
Large zipper-lock plastic bag
Rolling pin
Oven mitts

Rubber spatula
2 shallow dishes
1-tablespoon measuring spoon
Cooling rack

START BAKING!

1. Adjust oven rack to middle position and heat oven to 325 degrees. Line rimmed baking sheet with parchment paper.

2. In medium bowl, whisk together flour, cocoa, baking powder, baking soda, and salt. In large bowl, whisk brown sugar, egg and egg yolk, and vanilla until combined.

3. Place chocolate in large zipper-lock plastic bag and seal, removing as much air as possible from bag. Use rolling pin to gently pound chocolate into small pieces (see photo, page 111).

4. In small microwave-safe bowl, combine pounded chocolate and butter. Heat in microwave at 50 percent power (see page 11) until melted, 1 to 2 minutes. Use oven mitts to remove bowl from microwave. Use rubber spatula to stir chocolate mixture until well combined and shiny.

5. Add chocolate mixture to brown sugar mixture and use rubber spatula to stir until combined. Stir in flour mixture until no dry flour is visible. Let dough sit at room temperature for 10 minutes.

6. Place sugar in 1 shallow dish and confectioners' sugar in second shallow dish.

7. Use your hands to roll dough into 12 balls (about 2 tablespoons each). Drop balls directly into shallow dish with sugar and roll to coat. Transfer dough balls to shallow dish with confectioners' sugar and roll to evenly coat.

8. Place dough balls on parchment-lined baking sheet, leaving about 2 inches between balls (see photo, page 108).

9. Place baking sheet in oven. Bake cookies until puffed and cracked and edges have begun to set but centers are still soft (cookies will look raw in cracks and seem underdone), about 11 minutes.

10. Use oven mitts to remove baking sheet from oven (ask an adult for help). Place baking sheet on cooling rack and let cookies cool completely on baking sheet, about 30 minutes. Serve.

COOKIE 101

There are many different types of cookies, including two of our favorites: drop cookies and rolled cookies. We've put together tips and tricks to help you make the tastiest cookies, no matter which kind you bake!

COOKIE BASICS

Use these three simple tricks to achieve cookie perfection.

LINE SHEET

Line a rimmed baking sheet with parchment paper to prevent sticking.

STAGGER ROWS

Leave 2 inches between dough balls, arranging them in staggered rows so they do not spread into each other.

COOL ON SHEET

Leave cookies on baking sheet for at least 10 minutes so they can firm up, then transfer cookies directly to cooling rack.

STORING COOKIES AND BARS

COOKIES

Cookies can be stored in an airtight container for up to 2 days. To prevent cookies from turning dry and brittle, we recommend storing them in a zipper-lock bag with a half slice of sandwich bread.

BARS

Brownies can be stored in an airtight container for up to 2 days. Granola Bars can be stored in an airtight container for up to 1 week. Cheesecake Bars and Key Lime Bars can be stored in an airtight container in the refrigerator for up to 2 days.

DROP COOKIES

Drop cookies are American classics. Chocolate, oatmeal, peanut butter—these cookies typically have a lightly crisp outer edge and a soft, chewy middle. They are some of the easiest cookies to shape and bake.

  ## FORMING DROP COOKIES

Many recipes call for simply "dropping" (hence the name) a measurement of cookie dough onto the baking sheet, usually with two spoons. For the best cookies, we prefer to roll the dough between our hands into round balls. This creates cookies that are all the same shape and that bake evenly. With very soft doughs or sticky doughs (like our Oatmeal–Chocolate Chip Cookies, page 104) it's difficult to roll them between your hands, so we just drop them straight.

ROLLED COOKIES

Rolled (or cutout) cookies require a little more work to form than drop cookies. The dough can become too soft to roll or it can tear, and the thin cookies can overbake. Here are the keys to achieving great-tasting rolled cookies.

ROLL BETWEEN PARCHMENT

Rolling the cookie dough between 2 large sheets of parchment paper rather than on the counter minimizes sticking and makes it easier to transfer the cookies to the baking sheet; you simply remove the top piece of parchment, stamp out the cookies, and then transfer them to the baking sheet with a thin icing spatula instead of trying to get the cookies off the counter.

START ROLLING AT THE CENTER

When rolling out cookie dough, it helps to start at the center of the disk of dough and roll away from you, spinning the dough a quarter turn after each roll. This helps ensure every inch of dough is the same thickness. Try to apply even pressure as you roll.

CHEWY PEANUT BUTTER COOKIES

MAKES 12 COOKIES
TOTAL TIME: 35 MINUTES,
  PLUS 25 MINUTES COOLING TIME

PREPARE INGREDIENTS

¾ cup (3¾ ounces) all-purpose flour
½ teaspoon baking soda
¼ teaspoon salt
¼ cup dry-roasted peanuts
¾ cup packed (5¼ ounces) dark brown
  sugar
½ cup (4½ ounces) creamy peanut
  butter
1 large egg
2 tablespoons unsalted butter,
  melted and cooled (see page 13
  for how to melt butter)
1 tablespoon honey
½ teaspoon vanilla extract

GATHER BAKING EQUIPMENT

Rimmed baking sheet
Parchment paper
2 bowls (1 large, 1 medium)
Whisk
Large zipper-lock plastic bag
Rolling pin
Rubber spatula
1-tablespoon measuring spoon
Ruler
Oven mitts
Cooling rack
Spatula

"I like that it has a lot of nuts and nut flavor."
—Emery, 9

"These cookies were chewy in a nice way."
—Vivien, 11

START BAKING!

1. Adjust oven rack to middle position and heat oven to 350 degrees. Line rimmed baking sheet with parchment paper.

2. In medium bowl, whisk together flour, baking soda, and salt.

3. Place peanuts in large zipper-lock plastic bag and seal, removing as much air as possible from bag. Use rolling pin to gently pound peanuts into very small pieces (see photo, right).

4. In large bowl, use rubber spatula to stir brown sugar, peanut butter, egg, melted butter, honey, vanilla, and pounded peanuts until combined.

5. Add flour mixture to brown sugar mixture and use rubber spatula to stir until soft dough forms and no dry flour is visible.

6. Use your hands to roll dough into 12 balls (about 2 tablespoons each). Place dough balls on parchment-lined baking sheet, leaving space between balls (see photo, page 108). Use your fingers to gently flatten each dough ball into 2-inch-wide circle.

7. Place baking sheet in oven. Bake cookies until edges are just set, 10 to 12 minutes.

8. Use oven mitts to remove baking sheet from oven (ask an adult for help). Place baking sheet on cooling rack and let cookies cool on baking sheet for 10 minutes.

9. Use spatula to transfer cookies directly to cooling rack and let cookies cool completely, about 15 minutes. Serve.

CREAMY, CHEWY, PEANUTTY!

These cookies are chewy on the inside and slightly crisp around the edges, with big peanut butter flavor throughout. You probably already know that there are *many* different types of peanut butter: creamy, crunchy, natural, low-salt. Each has a different number and texture of peanuts, and often even different types of oil or other additives, which means that each kind of peanut butter gives cookies a different texture. For this recipe, be sure to use traditional creamy peanut butter for the best chewy peanut butter cookie. Our favorite is Skippy Creamy Peanut Butter.

KNIFE-FREE CHOPPING

Place nuts or bar chocolate in zipper-lock plastic bag. Seal bag, making sure to press out all air. Use rolling pin to gently pound bag to break nuts or chocolate into small pieces.

GIANT CHOCOLATE CHIP COOKIE

SERVES 12
TOTAL TIME: 45 MINUTES,
    PLUS 30 MINUTES COOLING TIME

PREPARE INGREDIENTS

Vegetable oil spray
1 cup (5 ounces) all-purpose flour
¼ teaspoon baking soda
¼ teaspoon salt
8 tablespoons unsalted butter, melted
    (see page 13 for how to melt butter)
½ cup packed (3½ ounces) dark brown sugar
¼ cup (1¾ ounces) sugar
1 large egg
1 teaspoon vanilla extract
½ cup (3 ounces) chocolate chips

GATHER BAKING EQUIPMENT

9-inch springform pan
2 bowls (1 large, 1 medium)
Whisk
Rubber spatula
Oven mitts
Cooling rack
Butter knife
Icing spatula or wide metal spatula
Cutting board
Chef's knife

TREAT YOUR COOKIE LIKE A CAKE

This cookie is so big, it's practically a cake! To make sure our giant cookie bakes up perfectly round, we use a round cake pan—specifically, a springform pan, which makes it easier to transfer the cookie and serve it since you can remove the side of the pan. If you don't have a springform pan, you can use a 9-inch round cake pan instead, but you'll have to flip the cookie out of the pan just like you would a cake. You can treat this cookie like a cake when serving, too: Slice it into wedges and serve it with Whipped Cream (see page 133) or a scoop of ice cream.

START BAKING!

1. Adjust oven rack to upper-middle position and heat oven to 375 degrees. Spray inside bottom and sides of 9-inch springform pan with vegetable oil spray.

2. In medium bowl, whisk together flour, baking soda, and salt.

3. In large bowl, whisk melted butter, brown sugar, and sugar until well combined. Add egg and vanilla and whisk until smooth.

4. Add flour mixture to butter mixture and use rubber spatula to stir until just combined and no dry flour is visible, about 1 minute. Add chocolate chips and stir until evenly distributed.

5. Use rubber spatula to scrape cookie dough into greased springform pan and spread dough into even layer covering bottom of pan (see photo, below).

6. Place springform pan in oven and bake until cookie is golden brown and edges are set, 18 to 22 minutes.

7. Use oven mitts to remove springform pan from oven (ask an adult for help). Place springform pan on cooling rack and let cookie cool in pan for 30 minutes.

8. Run butter knife around inside edge of springform pan to loosen edges of cookie from pan. Unlock and remove side of pan. Use icing spatula or wide metal spatula to loosen bottom of cookie from pan and transfer cookie to cutting board. Cut cookie into wedges and serve warm.

MAKING ONE GIANT COOKIE!

To ensure uniformly baked cookie, spread and press dough into even layer covering bottom of pan.

JAM THUMBPRINT COOKIES

MAKES 24 COOKIES
TOTAL TIME: 45 MINUTES,
PLUS 30 MINUTES COOLING TIME

PREPARE INGREDIENTS

1 cup plus 2 tablespoons (5⅔ ounces) all-purpose flour

¼ teaspoon salt

¼ teaspoon baking soda

⅛ teaspoon baking powder

6 tablespoons unsalted butter, cut into 6 pieces and softened (see page 13 for how to soften butter)

⅓ cup (2⅓ ounces) sugar

3 tablespoons (1½ ounces) cream cheese, softened

1 large egg yolk (see page 14 for how to separate eggs)

¾ teaspoon vanilla extract

⅓ cup jam (any flavor you want!)

GATHER BAKING EQUIPMENT

Rimmed baking sheet

Parchment paper

Medium bowl

Whisk

Electric mixer (stand mixer with paddle attachment or handheld mixer and large bowl)

Rubber spatula

1-teaspoon measuring spoon

½-teaspoon measuring spoon

Oven mitts

Cooling rack

MAKING THUMBPRINT COOKIES

1. Use your hands to roll dough into 24 balls (about 2 teaspoons each).

2. Use your thumb to make indentation in center of each dough ball.

3. Use ½-teaspoon measuring spoon to fill each hole with heaping ½ teaspoon jam.

START BAKING! ←≪≪≪

1. Adjust oven rack to middle position and heat oven to 350 degrees. Line rimmed baking sheet with parchment paper.

2. In medium bowl, whisk together flour, salt, baking soda, and baking powder.

3. In bowl of stand mixer (or large bowl if using handheld mixer), combine softened butter and sugar. If using stand mixer, lock bowl into place and attach paddle to stand mixer. Start mixer on medium-high speed and beat until fluffy, 3 to 4 minutes. Stop mixer and use rubber spatula to scrape down sides of bowl.

4. Add cream cheese, egg yolk, and vanilla. Start mixer on medium speed and beat until mixture is just combined, about 30 seconds. Stop mixer.

5. Carefully add flour mixture. Start mixer on low speed and beat until combined, about 30 seconds. Stop mixer. Remove bowl from stand mixer, if using.

6. Use your hands to roll dough into 24 balls (about 2 teaspoons each) (see photo, above). Place dough balls on parchment-lined baking sheet, leaving space between balls.

7. Shape and fill each cookie with jam (following photos, above).

8. Place baking sheet in oven. Bake cookies until light golden brown, 15 to 18 minutes.

9. Use oven mitts to remove baking sheet from oven (ask an adult for help). Place baking sheet on cooling rack and let cookies cool completely on baking sheet, about 30 minutes. Serve.

GLAZED SUGAR COOKIES

MAKES 12 TO 18 COOKIES (DEPENDING ON THE SIZE OF YOUR COOKIE CUTTERS)
TOTAL TIME: 50 MINUTES,
PLUS 1½ HOURS CHILLING TIME,
PLUS 30 MINUTES COOLING TIME

PREPARE INGREDIENTS

1½ cups (7½ ounces) all-purpose flour
⅛ teaspoon baking powder
⅛ teaspoon baking soda
¼ teaspoon salt
1 large egg
½ teaspoon vanilla extract
½ cup (3½ ounces) sugar
8 tablespoons unsalted butter, cut into 8 pieces and chilled (butter should be very cold!)
Spreadable Glaze (page 118)

GATHER BAKING EQUIPMENT

2 bowls (1 medium, 1 small)
Whisk
Food processor
Rubber spatula
Parchment paper
Ruler
Rolling pin
2 rimmed baking sheets

Cookie cutters
Spatula
Oven mitts
Cooling rack

"The best part for me was decorating the cookies, except eating them, of course."
—Christopher, 8

"The cookies had a really good crunch to them."
—Spencer, 10

1. In medium bowl, whisk together flour, baking powder, baking soda, and salt. In small bowl, whisk together egg and vanilla.

2. Add sugar to food processor and lock lid into place. Turn on processor and process until sugar is finely ground, about 30 seconds.

3. Stop processor and remove lid. Add chilled butter to processor and lock lid back into place. Turn on processor and process until smooth, about 30 seconds.

4. Stop processor and remove lid. Add egg mixture and flour mixture and lock lid back into place. Turn on processor and process until no dry flour is visible and mixture forms crumbly dough, about 30 seconds.

5. Stop processor, remove lid, and carefully remove processor blade (ask an adult for help). Use rubber spatula to transfer dough to center of large sheet of parchment paper on counter.

6. Use your hands to pat dough into 7-by-9-inch oval. Place second large sheet of parchment on top of dough. Use rolling pin to roll dough into 10-by-14-inch oval (⅛ to ¼ inch thick), rolling dough between parchment (see photo, page 109).

KEEP GOING! ⇝⟶

SAVE ALL YOUR SCRAPS!

After cutting out your cookie shapes in step 9, you can put all the leftover dough scraps together, reroll the dough between sheets of parchment paper to ⅛- to ¼-inch thickness, and cut out more shapes. It's best to do this only one time—if you reroll this dough more than once, the cookies will turn out tough.

7. Slide dough (still between parchment) onto 1 baking sheet. Place baking sheet in refrigerator and refrigerate until dough is firm, at least 1½ hours.

8. While dough is chilling, adjust oven rack to lower-middle position and heat oven to 300 degrees. Line second baking sheet with parchment.

9. When dough is ready, remove dough from refrigerator. Gently peel off top sheet of parchment. Use cookie cutters to cut dough into shapes. Use spatula to transfer shapes to parchment-lined baking sheet, spaced about ½ inch apart. (If dough becomes too warm and sticky to transfer shapes easily, return it to refrigerator to firm up again, about 10 minutes.)

10. Place baking sheet in oven. Bake cookies until beginning to brown around edges, 18 to 22 minutes.

11. Use oven mitts to remove baking sheet from oven (ask an adult for help). Place baking sheet on cooling rack and let cookies cool completely on baking sheet, about 30 minutes. Decorate as desired (see photos, right). Serve.

SPREADABLE GLAZE

One of our favorite ways to decorate cookies is with a glaze you can spread on with an icing spatula or back of a spoon. **To make glaze:** In medium bowl, combine 1⅓ cups (5⅓ ounces) confectioners' (powdered) sugar, 2 tablespoons milk, 1 tablespoon softened cream cheese, and 1 to 2 drops food coloring (if desired). Use rubber spatula to stir until very smooth. (See photo, right, for more on how to spread glaze.)

GLAZING AND DECORATING COOKIES

Glazing your cookies gives you a blank canvas for decorating. Just make sure to let the glaze dry completely, about 30 minutes, before serving.

1. Use small icing spatula or back of spoon to spread Spreadable Glaze (left) in even layer on cookie, starting in middle and working your way to edges.

2. While glaze is still wet, sprinkle with sanding sugar, sprinkles, crushed cookies, or candy.

SOFT AND CHEWY GINGERBREAD PEOPLE

MAKES 12 COOKIES
TOTAL TIME: 1 HOUR AND 20 MINUTES,
  PLUS 40 MINUTES COOLING TIME

PREPARE INGREDIENTS

1½ cups (7½ ounces) all-purpose flour
½ cup packed (3½ ounces) dark brown sugar
1½ teaspoons ground cinnamon
1½ teaspoons ground ginger
¼ teaspoon baking soda
¼ teaspoon salt
6 tablespoons unsalted butter,
  melted and cooled (see page 13
  for how to melt butter)
⅓ cup molasses
1 tablespoon (½ ounce) milk

GATHER BAKING EQUIPMENT

Food processor
Rubber spatula
Plastic wrap
Ruler
Rimmed baking
  sheet
Parchment paper
Rolling pin

3½-inch gingerbread
  person cookie
  cutter
Spatula
Oven mitts
Cooling rack

"Crunchy on the outside and soft on the inside."
—Lily, 11

"Yummy! The cookies were soft, chewy, and I-need-more-worthy!" —Brendan, 9

KNEADING COOKIE DOUGH

Transfer dough to clean counter. Knead dough until it forms smooth ball, about 20 seconds (it may stick to counter— if it does, use rubber spatula to get all dough off counter).

START BAKING! ← «««

1. Add flour, brown sugar, cinnamon, ginger, baking soda, and salt to food processor and lock lid into place. Turn on processor and process until combined, about 10 seconds.

2. Stop processor and remove lid. Add melted butter, molasses, and milk and lock lid back into place. Turn on processor and process until soft and crumbly dough forms and no streaks of flour remain, about 20 seconds.

3. Stop processor, remove lid, and carefully remove processor blade (ask an adult for help). Use rubber spatula to scrape dough onto clean counter. Knead dough until it comes together, about 20 seconds (it may stick to counter—if it does, use rubber spatula to get all dough off counter) (see photo, left).

4. Lay sheet of plastic wrap on counter. Place dough in center of plastic and flatten dough into 8-inch circle. Wrap dough tightly in plastic and refrigerate for at least 30 minutes or up to 24 hours. If dough has been refrigerated for more than 1 hour, be sure to let dough sit on counter for 15 minutes before rolling out.

5. Adjust oven rack to middle position and heat oven to 350 degrees. Line rimmed baking sheet with parchment paper.

6. Remove dough from refrigerator and discard plastic. Place dough in center of second large sheet of parchment. Place third large sheet of parchment on top of dough. Use rolling pin to roll dough into 11-inch circle (about ¼ inch thick), rolling dough between parchment (see photo, page 109).

7. Peel off top sheet of parchment. Use cookie cutter to cut dough into gingerbread people. Use spatula to transfer shapes to parchment-lined baking sheet, spaced about ½ inch apart.

8. Gather dough scraps and place them in center of large piece of parchment, and place another piece of parchment on top. Repeat rolling and cutting steps with dough scraps until you have 12 cookies. Discard remaining dough scraps.

9. Place baking sheet in oven. Bake until cookies are slightly puffy and just set around edges, 9 to 11 minutes.

10. Use oven mitts to remove baking sheet from oven (ask an adult for help). Place baking sheet on cooling rack and let cookies cool on baking sheet for 10 minutes.

11. Use spatula to transfer cookies directly to cooling rack. Let cookies cool completely, about 30 minutes. Decorate as desired (see Spreadable Glaze, page 118, and Glazing and Decorating Cookies, page 119). Serve.

MEXICAN WEDDING COOKIES

MAKES 24 COOKIES
TOTAL TIME: 50 MINUTES,
    PLUS 20 MINUTES COOLING TIME

PREPARE INGREDIENTS

1 cup (4 ounces) walnuts or pecans
1 cup (5 ounces) all-purpose flour
½ teaspoon salt
8 tablespoons unsalted butter,
    cut into 8 pieces and softened
    (see page 13 for how to soften butter)
¼ cup (1¾ ounces) sugar
¾ teaspoon vanilla extract
¾ cup (3 ounces) confectioners'
    (powdered) sugar

GATHER BAKING EQUIPMENT

Rimmed baking sheet
Parchment paper
Large zipper-lock plastic bag
Rolling pin
Medium bowl
Whisk
Electric mixer (stand mixer with paddle
    attachment or handheld mixer and
    large bowl)
Rubber spatula
1-tablespoon measuring spoon
Oven mitts
Cooling rack
Shallow dish

A COOKIE WITH MANY NAMES

Mexican Wedding Cakes, Nut Crescents, Viennese Crescents, Butterballs, Russian Tea Cakes, Swedish Tea Cakes, Italian Butter Nuts, Southern Pecan Butterballs, Snowdrops, Viennese Sugar Balls, Sand Tarts, and Snowballs... These are all names for the same type of cookie—this one! People have been baking them all over the world for generations. Light, buttery, nutty, and tender, these cookies are delicious by any name.

START BAKING!

1. Adjust oven rack to middle position and heat oven to 325 degrees. Line rimmed baking sheet with parchment paper.

2. Place walnuts in large zipper-lock plastic bag and seal, removing as much air as possible from bag. Use rolling pin to gently pound walnuts into very small pieces (see photo, page 111).

3. In medium bowl, whisk together pounded walnuts, flour, and salt.

4. Add softened butter and sugar to bowl of stand mixer (or large bowl if using handheld mixer). If using stand mixer, lock bowl into place and attach paddle to stand mixer. Start mixer on medium-high speed and beat until pale and fluffy, 3 to 4 minutes. Stop mixer and use rubber spatula to scrape down sides of bowl.

5. Add vanilla and flour mixture. Start mixer on low speed and mix until combined, about 45 seconds. Stop mixer. Remove bowl from stand mixer, if using. Use rubber spatula to scrape down sides of bowl and stir in any remaining dry flour.

6. Use your hands to roll dough into 24 balls (about 1 tablespoon each). Place dough balls on parchment-lined baking sheet, leaving space between balls.

7. Place baking sheet in oven. Bake cookies until tops are pale golden and bottoms are just beginning to brown, about 18 minutes.

8. Use oven mitts to remove baking sheet from oven (ask an adult for help). Place baking sheet on cooling rack and let cookies cool completely on baking sheet, about 20 minutes.

9. Spread confectioners' sugar in shallow dish. Working with 4 cookies at a time, roll cookies in confectioners' sugar to coat (see photo, below). Just before serving, reroll cookies in confectioners' sugar a second time.

COATING YOUR COOKIES

To ensure a thorough, even coating of confectioners' sugar (with no bald spots), we like to roll the cookies in the sugar two times!

Working with 4 cookies at a time, roll cookies in confectioners' sugar to coat. Just before serving, reroll cookies in confectioners' sugar.

COCONUT MACAROONS

MAKES 18 COOKIES
TOTAL TIME: 1 HOUR,
    PLUS 40 MINUTES COOLING TIME

PREPARE INGREDIENTS

Vegetable oil spray
½ cup (5½ ounces) cream of coconut
2 large egg whites (see page 14
    for how to separate eggs)
1 teaspoon vanilla extract
¼ teaspoon salt
1½ cups (4½ ounces) unsweetened
    shredded coconut
1½ cups (4½ ounces) sweetened
    shredded coconut

GATHER BAKING EQUIPMENT

Rimmed baking sheet
Parchment paper
2 bowls (1 large, 1 medium)
Whisk
Rubber spatula
1-tablespoon measuring spoon
Oven mitts
Cooling rack
Spatula

"It was simple and fun to make
and they were delicious when
they were done." —Macey, 10

THREE TYPES OF COCONUT

Coconut comes in many forms—there's sweetened and unsweetened shredded coconut, coconut milk, cream of coconut (not to be confused with coconut cream!), and coconut water, to name a few. To make these cookies as coconutty as possible, we use three different types of coconut. A mix of sweetened and unsweetened shredded coconut gives them good coconut texture and flavor (and balances the sweetness—it turns out there is such a thing as too sweet!). Plus, the cream of coconut adds moisture, creaminess, and even more coconut flavor. Bonus: with just egg whites to keep it all together, these cookies are naturally gluten-free.

1. Adjust oven rack to middle position and heat oven to 325 degrees. Line rimmed baking sheet with parchment paper. Spray parchment with vegetable oil spray.

2. In medium bowl, whisk cream of coconut, egg whites, vanilla, and salt until combined.

3. In large bowl, combine unsweetened and sweetened shredded coconut, breaking up clumps with your fingertips. Add cream of coconut mixture and use rubber spatula to stir until coconut is evenly moistened. Refrigerate dough for 15 minutes.

4. Use 1-tablespoon measuring spoon to scoop, drop, and shape 18 cookies (following photos, right).

5. Place baking sheet in oven. Bake until cookies are light golden brown, 18 to 22 minutes.

6. Use oven mitts to remove baking sheet from oven (ask an adult for help). Place baking sheet on cooling rack and let cookies cool on baking sheet for 10 minutes.

7. Use spatula to transfer cookies directly to cooling rack and let cool completely, about 30 minutes. Serve.

SHAPING MACAROONS

1. Use 1-tablespoon measuring spoon to drop dough onto parchment-lined baking sheet in 18 mounds (about 1 heaping tablespoon each), leaving space between mounds.

2. Using wet fingertips, shape mounds into pyramids, rewetting your fingertips as necessary to prevent sticking.

CHEWY BROWNIES

MAKES 16 BROWNIES
TOTAL TIME: 55 MINUTES, PLUS 1½ HOURS
   COOLING TIME

PREPARE INGREDIENTS

Vegetable oil spray
1 ounce unsweetened chocolate
3 tablespoons Dutch-processed cocoa powder
⅓ cup (2⅔ ounces) water
5 tablespoons vegetable oil
2 tablespoons unsalted butter, melted and
   cooled (see page 13 for how to melt butter)
1¼ cups (8¾ ounces) sugar
1 large egg plus 1 large egg yolk (see page 14
   for how to separate eggs)
1 teaspoon vanilla extract
¾ cup plus 2 tablespoons (4⅜ ounces)
   all-purpose flour
½ cup (3 ounces) bittersweet chocolate chips
½ teaspoon salt

GATHER BAKING EQUIPMENT

Aluminum foil
8-inch square metal baking pan
Ruler
Large zipper-lock plastic bag
Rolling pin
Large bowl
Liquid measuring cup
Oven mitts
Whisk
Rubber spatula
Toothpick
Cooling rack
Cutting board
Chef's knife

WHAT MAKES A BROWNIE CHEWY?

We love the chewy texture of brownies that come from a boxed mix, and we wanted to re-create it—without the boxed mix. The solution turned out to need just a little bit of math. The secret to a boxed-mix brownie's chewy texture boils down to one thing: fat—specifically, the ratio of saturated fat (butter) to unsaturated fat (vegetable oil). By using roughly one-third as much butter as vegetable oil, we got the exact chewy texture we wanted. No boxed mix needed!

START BAKING!

1. Adjust oven rack to lowest position and heat oven to 350 degrees. Make aluminum foil sling for 8-inch square metal baking pan (following photos, page 15). Spray foil with vegetable oil spray.

2. Place chocolate in large zipper-lock plastic bag and seal, removing as much air as possible from bag. Use rolling pin to gently pound chocolate into small pieces (see photo, page 111).

3. In large bowl, combine cocoa and pounded chocolate.

4. Heat water in liquid measuring cup in microwave until hot, 1 to 1½ minutes. Use oven mitts to remove measuring cup from microwave. Pour hot water over cocoa mixture and carefully whisk until chocolate is melted and smooth.

5. Whisk in oil and melted butter (mixture will look lumpy and separated). Whisk in sugar, egg and egg yolk, and vanilla until smooth. Add flour, chocolate chips, and salt and use rubber spatula to stir until combined and no dry flour is visible.

6. Use rubber spatula to scrape batter into foil-lined baking pan and smooth top.

7. Place baking pan in oven. Bake until toothpick inserted in center comes out with few moist crumbs attached (see photo, page 15), 25 to 28 minutes.

8. Use oven mitts to remove baking pan from oven (ask an adult for help). Place baking pan on cooling rack and let brownies cool completely in pan, about 1½ hours.

9. Use foil to carefully lift brownies out of baking pan and place on cutting board. Cut into squares and serve.

CHEWY GRANOLA BARS WITH CRANBERRIES AND WALNUTS

MAKES 12 BARS
TOTAL TIME: 1¼ HOURS, PLUS 2 HOURS COOLING TIME

PREPARE INGREDIENTS

"This would be a great snack to have when I get home from school!" —Victoria, 13

Vegetable oil spray
¾ cup (3 ounces) walnuts
1¼ cups (3¾ ounces) old-fashioned rolled oats (see page 105)
½ cup raw sunflower seeds
¼ cup vegetable oil
2 tablespoons (1 ounce) water
½ cup dried apricots
½ cup packed (3½ ounces) brown sugar
¼ teaspoon salt
¾ cup (¾ ounce) Rice Krispies cereal
½ cup dried cranberries

GATHER BAKING EQUIPMENT

Aluminum foil
8-inch square metal baking pan
Ruler
Food processor
Rubber spatula
Rimmed baking sheet

Oven mitts
Cooling rack
Liquid measuring cup
Large bowl
Dry measuring cup
Cutting board
Chef's knife

START BAKING!

1. Adjust oven rack to middle position and heat oven to 350 degrees. Make aluminum foil sling for 8-inch square metal baking pan (following photos, page 15). Spray foil with vegetable oil spray.

2. Add walnuts to food processor and lock lid into place. Hold down pulse button for 1 second, then release. Repeat until walnuts are finely chopped, about ten 1-second pulses.

3. Remove lid and carefully remove processor blade (ask an adult for help). Use rubber spatula to transfer walnuts to rimmed baking sheet. Add oats and sunflower seeds to baking sheet and use rubber spatula to spread into even layer.

4. Place baking sheet in oven and bake until oats are lightly browned, about 12 minutes.

5. Use oven mitts to remove baking sheet from oven (ask an adult for help). Place baking sheet on cooling rack and let cool for 10 minutes. While oat mixture is cooling, reduce oven temperature to 300 degrees.

6. Combine oil and water in liquid measuring cup. Add apricots, brown sugar, and salt to food processor and lock lid back into place. Turn on processor and process until apricots are very finely ground, about 15 seconds.

7. With processor running, pour oil mixture through feed tube and process until paste forms, about 1 minute. Stop processor.

8. Remove lid and carefully remove processor blade (ask an adult for help). Use rubber spatula to transfer apricot paste to large bowl. Add cooled oat mixture and use rubber spatula to stir until oats are well coated with apricot paste. Add cereal and cranberries and gently stir until evenly combined.

9. Use rubber spatula to scrape mixture into foil-lined baking pan and spread into even layer. Use bottom of dry measuring cup to press down VERY firmly (especially at edges and corners) until smooth and flat.

10. Place baking pan in oven and bake until granola is brown at edges, about 25 minutes.

11. Use oven mitts to remove baking pan from oven (ask an adult for help). Place baking pan on cooling rack and let granola bars cool completely in pan, about 2 hours.

12. Use foil to lift bars out of baking pan and transfer to cutting board. Cut into bars and serve.

KEY LIME BARS

MAKES 16 BARS
TOTAL TIME: 1¼ HOURS, PLUS 4 HOURS COOLING AND CHILLING TIME

PREPARE INGREDIENTS

Crust

Vegetable oil spray

5 whole graham crackers, broken into pieces (or ¾ cup store-bought graham cracker crumbs)

⅓ cup (1⅔ ounces) all-purpose flour

¼ cup (1¾ ounces) sugar

⅛ teaspoon salt

4 tablespoons unsalted butter, melted (see page 13 for how to melt butter)

Filling

1 (14-ounce) can sweetened condensed milk

¼ cup (2 ounces) cream cheese, softened

1 tablespoon grated lime zest plus ½ cup juice (zested and squeezed from 4 limes) (see page 17 for how to zest and juice limes)

1 large egg yolk (see page 14 for how to separate eggs)

Pinch salt

½ cup (1½ ounces) sweetened shredded coconut, toasted (see page 132), optional

Whipped Cream (page 133), optional

GATHER BAKING EQUIPMENT

Aluminum foil
8-inch square metal baking pan
Ruler
Food processor
Rubber spatula
Dry measuring cup
Oven mitts
Cooling rack
Large bowl
Whisk
Plastic wrap
Cutting board
Chef's knife

1. **For the crust:** Adjust oven rack to middle position and heat oven to 325 degrees. Make aluminum foil sling for 8-inch square metal baking pan (following photos, page 15). Spray foil with vegetable oil spray.

2. Add cracker pieces, flour, sugar, and ⅛ teaspoon salt to food processor and lock lid into place. Hold down pulse button for 1 second, then release. Repeat until crackers are broken into small pieces, about five 1-second pulses.

3. Turn on processor and process until crackers are finely ground, about 30 seconds. Stop processor. Remove lid, add melted butter to processor, and lock lid back into place. Pulse until butter is combined with crumbs, about ten 1-second pulses.

4. Remove lid and carefully remove processor blade (ask an adult for help). Use rubber spatula to scrape crumb mixture into foil-lined baking pan.

5. Use your hands to press crumbs into even layer covering bottom of baking pan, then use bottom of dry measuring cup to press crumbs firmly into pan until very flat (see photo, page 133).

6. Place baking pan in oven. Bake until crust begins to brown at edges, 15 to 20 minutes.

7. Use oven mitts to remove baking pan from oven (ask an adult for help). Place baking pan on cooling rack and let crust cool for at least 15 minutes. (Do not turn off oven.)

KEEP GOING! ⋙⟶

WHAT ARE KEY LIMES, ANYWAY?

Key limes are smaller, yellower cousins to the bigger, darker green Persian limes you usually see in the grocery store. Key limes are more tart, with fragrant, floral juice. They used to be grown widely in the Florida Keys, and cooks who lived there invented key lime pie as a way to use the juice. But to make these Key Lime Bars, you don't need key limes—they can be hard to find and are so small that you'd have to squeeze 20 of them to get ½ cup of juice! Regular Persian limes work just fine, but whatever you do, don't use bottled lime juice in this recipe (fresh juice has much better flavor!).

TOASTED COCONUT

Toasted coconut is a great addition to baked goods such as cookies or bars or as a topping for ice cream or oatmeal. It can sometimes burn when you toast it in the oven, so we like to use the microwave, where you can keep a close eye on it as it cooks.

To make toasted coconut: Spread ½ cup sweetened shredded coconut into even layer on large plate. Cook in microwave until golden brown, 3 to 5 minutes, stopping to stir with rubber spatula every 30 seconds. Use oven mitts to remove plate from microwave (careful—plate will be HOT!) and let cool to room temperature.

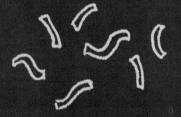

8. **For the filling:** Meanwhile, in large bowl, whisk condensed milk, softened cream cheese, lime zest and juice, egg yolk, and pinch salt until well combined and smooth.

9. Pour filling evenly over cooled crust. Use clean rubber spatula to scrape all filling from bowl. Spread filling into even layer to corners of pan and smooth top.

10. Place baking pan in oven and bake until filling is set and no longer jiggles when pan is shaken gently (ask an adult for help), 15 to 20 minutes.

11. Use oven mitts to remove baking pan from oven (ask an adult for help). Place baking pan on cooling rack and let bars cool in pan for 2 hours. Cover baking pan with plastic wrap and refrigerate until bars are chilled and firm, at least 2 hours or up to 2 days.

12. Remove bars from refrigerator and remove plastic. Use foil to lift bars out of baking pan and transfer to cutting board. Cut into squares. Top squares with toasted coconut or Whipped Cream (if using) and serve.

WHIPPED CREAM

For great whipped cream, heavy or whipping cream is a must. And make sure the cream is cold. Use an electric mixer for fastest results, although you can use a whisk and whip cream by hand—just be prepared for a workout! If using a mixer, keep the beaters low in the bowl to minimize splatters. This recipe makes about 1 cup. (To make 2 cups, double all ingredients.)

To make Whipped Cream: In large bowl, combine ½ cup cold heavy cream, 1½ teaspoons sugar, and ½ teaspoon vanilla extract. Use electric mixer on medium-low speed to whip cream for 1 minute. Increase speed to high and whip until cream is smooth and thick, about 1 minute. Stop mixer and lift beaters out of cream. If cream clings to the beaters and makes soft peaks that stand up on their own, you're done. If not, keep beating and check again in 30 seconds. Don't overwhip cream.

MAKING A BAR CRUST

Use your hands to press crumbs into even layer covering bottom of baking pan. Then use bottom of dry measuring cup to press crumbs firmly into pan to make flat surface.

CHEESECAKE BARS

MAKES 16 BARS
TOTAL TIME: 1½ HOURS, PLUS 6 HOURS
   COOLING AND CHILLING TIME

PREPARE INGREDIENTS

Crust
Vegetable oil spray
5 whole graham crackers, broken into
   pieces (or ¾ cup store-bought graham
   cracker crumbs)
⅓ cup (1⅔ ounces) all-purpose flour
⅛ teaspoon salt
¼ cup (1¾ ounces) sugar
4 tablespoons unsalted butter, melted
   (see page 13 for how to melt butter)

Filling
1 pound cream cheese
¾ cup (5¼ ounces) sugar
2 large eggs
1½ teaspoons vanilla extract
1 recipe Easy Strawberry Topping
   (see page 136), optional

GATHER BAKING EQUIPMENT

Aluminum foil
8-inch square metal baking pan
Ruler
Food processor
Rubber spatula
Dry measuring cup
Oven mitts

Cooling rack
Plastic wrap
Cutting board
Chef's knife

"It was very fun to make, especially to see the cream cheese get mixed in." —Aurelia, 11

"I loved it! It was gone super fast." —Zoe, 9

1. **For the crust:** Adjust oven rack to middle position and heat oven to 300 degrees. Make aluminum foil sling for 8-inch square metal baking pan (following photos, page 15). Spray foil with vegetable oil spray.

2. Add cracker pieces, flour, salt, and ¼ cup sugar to food processor and lock lid into place. Hold down pulse button for 1 second, then release. Repeat until crackers are broken into small pieces, about five 1-second pulses.

3. Turn on processor and process until crackers are finely ground, about 30 seconds. Stop processor. Remove lid, add melted butter to processor, and lock lid back into place. Pulse until butter is combined with crumbs, about ten 1-second pulses.

4. Remove lid and carefully remove processor blade (ask an adult for help). Use rubber spatula to scrape mixture into foil-lined baking pan.

5. Use your hands to press crumbs into even layer covering bottom of baking pan, then use bottom of dry measuring cup to press crumbs firmly into pan until very flat (see photo, page 133).

6. Place baking pan in oven. Bake until crust begins to brown at edges, 15 to 20 minutes.

7. Use oven mitts to remove baking pan from oven (ask an adult for help). Place baking pan on cooling rack and let crust cool for at least 15 minutes. (Do not turn off oven.)

KEEP GOING! ≫≫≫→

A PIECE OF CAKE

Cheesecake is delicious, but baking a big traditional one can be tricky. You have to bake a large cheesecake inside another pan filled with water to make sure it bakes evenly—a fussy and delicate maneuver in the oven. Smaller cheesecake bars are just as delicious, with a crisp graham cracker crust and a tangy, custardy filling, and are much easier to make (no water bath required). Plus, they are portable and easy to share—perfect for bake sales, parties, or any occasion!

EASY STRAWBERRY TOPPING

Fresh berries are a great topping for baked goods such as Cheesecake Bars (page 134), Pound Cake (page 150), Olive Oil Cake (page 178), or Individual Flourless Chocolate Cakes (page 184), but tossing strawberries with sugar (called macerating) takes it to the next level. The sugar draws out juice from the berries and turns them a bright ruby red.

To make strawberry topping: Use paring knife to hull 2 cups (10 ounces) strawberries (see photo, below). Slice strawberries and place in medium bowl. Add 1 tablespoon sugar and use spoon to stir until combined. Let sit until sugar has dissolved and strawberries are juicy, at least 30 minutes or up to 2 hours. Spoon over your favorite baked good or ice cream!

8. For the cheesecake filling: Add cream cheese and ¾ cup sugar to clean, dry food processor and lock lid back into place. Turn on processor and process until smooth, about 3 minutes.

9. With processor running, add eggs and vanilla through feed tube and process until just combined, about 30 seconds. Stop processor. Remove lid and carefully remove processor blade (ask an adult for help).

10. Pour filling evenly over cooled crust, using rubber spatula to scrape out all filling from food processor bowl.

11. Place baking pan in oven and bake until edges are set and puffed slightly but center still jiggles slightly when baking pan is shaken (ask an adult for help), 30 to 35 minutes.

12. Use oven mitts to remove baking pan from oven (ask an adult for help). Place baking pan on cooling rack and let bars cool in pan for 2 hours. Cover baking pan with plastic wrap and refrigerate until bars are chilled and firm, at least 4 hours or up to 2 days.

13. Remove baking pan from refrigerator and remove plastic. Use foil to lift bars out of baking pan and transfer to cutting board. Cut into squares. Top each square with strawberry topping (if using). Serve.

CHAPTER 5: CAKES & CUPCAKES

THERE ARE CAKES TO MAKE FOR EVERY OCCASION—
FROM AFTER-SCHOOL SNACKING TO SLEEPOVER ADVENTURING
AND CELEBRATING WITH FAMILY AND FRIENDS.

BERRY SNACK CAKE

SERVES 12

TOTAL TIME: 1 HOUR AND 10 MINUTES,
  PLUS 2 HOURS COOLING TIME

PREPARE INGREDIENTS

Vegetable oil spray
1½ cups (7½ ounces) all-purpose flour
1½ teaspoons baking powder
½ teaspoon salt
8 tablespoons unsalted butter, cut into
  8 pieces and softened (see page 13
  for how to soften butter)
⅔ cup packed (4⅔ ounces) light brown
  sugar
2 large eggs
1 teaspoon vanilla extract
⅓ cup (2⅔ ounces) whole milk
¾ cup (3¾ ounces) blueberries
¾ cup (3¾ ounces) raspberries

GATHER BAKING EQUIPMENT

8-inch square metal baking pan
8-inch square piece of parchment paper
  (see page 146)
Medium bowl
Whisk
Electric mixer (stand mixer with paddle
  attachment or handheld mixer and
  large bowl)
Rubber spatula
Toothpick
Oven mitts
Cooling rack
Cutting board
Chef's knife

BRIGHT AND BEAUTIFUL

This pretty, simple snack cake is perfect for after school (or even for breakfast, if you're in need of a special morning treat). The blueberries and raspberries add bright color and fresh flavor. You can substitute frozen berries for fresh if you like. Just thaw them before using!

START BAKING!

1. Adjust oven rack to middle position and heat oven to 350 degrees. Spray inside bottom and sides of 8-inch square metal baking pan with vegetable oil spray. Line bottom of baking pan with 8-inch square piece of parchment paper.

2. In medium bowl, whisk together flour, baking powder, and salt.

3. In bowl of stand mixer (or large bowl if using handheld mixer), combine softened butter and sugar. Lock bowl into place and attach paddle to stand mixer, if using. Start mixer on medium-high speed. Beat until mixture is light and fluffy, 3 to 4 minutes. Stop mixer.

4. Use rubber spatula to scrape down sides of bowl. Add eggs and vanilla. Start mixer on medium speed and beat until combined, about 30 seconds. Stop mixer.

5. Carefully add half of flour mixture. Start mixer on low speed and mix until combined, about 30 seconds. With mixer running, slowly pour in milk and mix until combined, about 30 seconds. Stop mixer.

6. Add remaining flour mixture. Start mixer on low speed and mix until well combined, about 30 seconds. Stop mixer. Remove bowl from stand mixer, if using.

7. Use rubber spatula to scrape down sides of bowl and stir in any remaining dry flour (batter will be very thick). Add blueberries and raspberries and use rubber spatula to gently stir until just combined.

8. Use rubber spatula to scrape batter into parchment-lined baking pan and smooth top (make sure to spread batter into corners to create even layer).

9. Place baking pan in oven. Bake until cake is golden brown and toothpick inserted in center comes out clean (see photo, page 15), 30 to 35 minutes.

10. Use oven mitts to remove baking pan from oven (ask an adult for help). Place baking pan on cooling rack and let cake cool completely in pan, about 2 hours.

11. Remove cake from baking pan and discard parchment (following photos, page 147). Cut cake into pieces and serve.

"I thought it was the best cake I've ever had in my life. The mayo made it so moist it melted in my mouth!"—Henry, 9

"I really liked the cake! I hate mayonnaise, but I loved this mayonnaise cake!"—Carly, 11

EASY CHOCOLATE SNACK CAKE

SERVES 12
TOTAL TIME: 1 HOUR AND 10 MINUTES, PLUS 2 HOURS COOLING TIME

PREPARE INGREDIENTS

Vegetable oil spray
1½ cups (7½ ounces) all-purpose flour
1 cup (7 ounces) sugar
½ teaspoon baking soda
¼ teaspoon salt
½ cup (1½ ounces) Dutch-processed
  cocoa powder
⅓ cup (2 ounces) chocolate chips
1 cup (8 ounces) water
⅔ cup mayonnaise
1 large egg
2 teaspoons vanilla extract
Confectioners' (powdered) sugar
  (optional)

GATHER BAKING EQUIPMENT

8-inch square metal baking pan
8-inch square piece of parchment
  paper (see page 146)
2 bowls (1 large, 1 medium)
Whisk
Liquid measuring cup
Oven mitts
Rubber spatula
Toothpick
Cooling rack
Small fine-mesh strainer for dusting
  with sugar
Cutting board
Chef's knife

1. Adjust oven rack to middle position and heat oven to 350 degrees. Spray inside bottom and sides of 8-inch square metal baking pan with vegetable oil spray. Line bottom of baking pan with 8-inch square piece of parchment paper.

2. In medium bowl, whisk together flour, sugar, baking soda, and salt. In large bowl, combine cocoa and chocolate chips.

3. Heat water in liquid measuring cup in microwave until hot and steaming, 1 to 2 minutes. Use oven mitts to remove measuring cup from microwave. Carefully pour water over chocolate mixture and whisk until smooth. Let mixture cool for 10 minutes.

4. Add mayonnaise, egg, and vanilla to cooled chocolate mixture and whisk until combined. Add flour mixture and use rubber spatula to stir until just combined and no dry flour remains.

5. Use rubber spatula to scrape batter into parchment-lined baking pan and smooth top (make sure to spread batter into corners to create even layer).

6. Place baking pan in oven. Bake until toothpick inserted in center of cake comes out clean (see photo, page 15), 34 to 38 minutes.

7. Use oven mitts to remove baking pan from oven (ask an adult for help). Place baking pan on cooling rack and let cake cool completely in pan, about 2 hours.

8. Remove cake from baking pan and discard parchment (following photos, page 147). Dust cake with confectioners' sugar (following photos, page 217). Cut cake into pieces and serve.

MAYONNAISE IN A CAKE?

Using mayonnaise as an ingredient in this recipe seemed strange to us at first, too. But then we remembered that mayonnaise is mostly made from two common cake ingredients: egg yolks and oil! (Mayo also contains an acid such as vinegar or lemon juice.) Two-thirds of a cup of mayonnaise is the trick to making this cake super moist and delicious. And you might already have this key ingredient in your refrigerator or pantry.

TAHINI-BANANA SNACK CAKE

SERVES 12
TOTAL TIME: 1½ HOURS,
    PLUS 2 HOURS COOLING TIME

PREPARE INGREDIENTS

Vegetable oil spray
1½ cups (7½ ounces) all-purpose flour
½ teaspoon salt
½ teaspoon baking soda
3 very ripe bananas (skins should be speckled black)
4 tablespoons unsalted butter, cut into 4 pieces and
    softened (see page 13 for how to soften butter)
1¼ cups (8¾ ounces) sugar
⅓ cup tahini
2 large eggs
¾ teaspoon vanilla extract
¼ cup (2 ounces) whole milk
2 teaspoons sesame seeds

GATHER BAKING EQUIPMENT

8-inch square metal baking pan
8-inch square piece of parchment paper
    (see page 146)
2 bowls (1 large, 1 medium)
Whisk
Large fork or potato masher
1-cup dry measuring cup
Electric mixer (stand mixer with paddle
    attachment or handheld mixer and large bowl)
Rubber spatula
Toothpick
Oven mitts
Cooling rack
Cutting board
Chef's knife

OPEN SESAME

You know peanut butter, but have you tried tahini? While peanut butter is made by grinding up peanuts, tahini is a paste made by grinding up toasted sesame seeds and is a popular ingredient in Middle Eastern cuisine (think hummus). Just be sure to stir it up before measuring!

START BAKING!

1. Adjust oven rack to middle position and heat oven to 350 degrees. Spray inside bottom and sides of 8-inch square metal baking pan with vegetable oil spray. Line bottom of baking pan with 8-inch square piece of parchment paper.

2. In medium bowl, whisk together flour, salt, and baking soda.

3. Peel bananas and place in large bowl. Use large fork or potato masher to mash bananas until broken down but still chunky. Measure out 1 cup mashed bananas (discard any extra).

4. In bowl of stand mixer (or large bowl if using handheld mixer), combine softened butter, sugar, and tahini. Lock bowl into place and attach paddle to stand mixer, if using. Start mixer on medium-high speed. Beat until mixture is light and fluffy, 3 to 4 minutes.

5. Add eggs and beat until combined, about 30 seconds. Add mashed bananas and vanilla and beat until incorporated, about 30 seconds. Stop mixer.

6. Carefully add half of flour mixture. Start mixer on low speed and mix until combined, about 1 minute. With mixer running, slowly pour in milk and mix until combined, about 30 seconds. Stop mixer.

7. Add remaining flour mixture. Start mixer on low speed and mix until well combined, about 1 minute. Stop mixer. Remove bowl from stand mixer, if using.

8. Use rubber spatula to scrape down sides of bowl and stir in any remaining dry flour. Use rubber spatula to scrape batter into parchment-lined baking pan and smooth top (make sure to spread batter into corners to create even layer). Sprinkle sesame seeds over top.

9. Place baking pan in oven. Bake until cake is deep golden brown and toothpick inserted in center comes out clean (see photo, page 15), 40 to 50 minutes.

10. Use oven mitts to remove baking pan from oven (ask an adult for help). Place baking pan on cooling rack and let cake cool completely in pan, about 2 hours.

11. Remove cake from baking pan and discard parchment (following photos, page 147). Cut cake into pieces and serve.

CAKE PREP 101

Cakes come in all shapes and sizes, but most benefit from the same couple of prep steps. Follow these tricks to help get your cake out of the pan, and make sure you store your leftovers for maximum deliciousness.

HOW TO LINE A CAKE PAN WITH PARCHMENT PAPER

To help remove cakes from their pans, we often line the pan with parchment paper before baking. Otherwise, the cake could stick and break into pieces as you attempt to remove it!

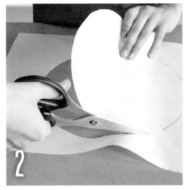

1. Place cake pan on sheet of parchment paper and trace around bottom of pan.

2. Cut out parchment with scissors.

3. Then place parchment into greased pan.

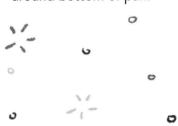

HOW TO REMOVE CAKES FROM PANS

Some cakes cool completely in their pans, while others need to be removed while they are still warm so they can cool on wire cooling racks. Ask an adult for help if the cake is still warm.

1. Run butter knife around edge of cake to release cake from pan.

2. Place cooling rack on top of cake. Hold bottom of cake pan with one hand (use oven mitt if pan is still hot) and place second hand on top of cooling rack. Turn over pan so cake falls gently onto rack.

3. Carefully peel parchment paper away from cake and discard. Place cutting board or serving platter on top of cake and flip cake right side up onto cutting board or serving platter.

4. Remove cooling rack.

HOW TO STORE CAKES

Snack Cakes: Cooled cakes can be wrapped in plastic wrap and stored at room temperature for up to 24 hours.

Sheet Cakes, Layer Cakes, Cupcakes, and Tea Cakes: Cooled, unfrosted cakes can be wrapped in plastic wrap and stored at room temperature for up to 24 hours. Once frosted (or glazed), cakes can be refrigerated for up to 24 hours; let cakes come to room temperature before serving.

Pound Cake and Olive Oil Cake: Cooled cakes can be wrapped in plastic wrap and stored at room temperature for up to 3 days.

"We loved the molasses flavor! The cake was easy to make, and our entire family loved it!" —Alexis, 9

"I really love how you put the ingredients in order of use. It makes making the recipe so much easier." —Mackenzie, 11

GINGERBREAD SNACK CAKE

SERVES 12
TOTAL TIME: 1 HOUR AND 10 MINUTES, PLUS 1½ HOURS COOLING TIME

PREPARE INGREDIENTS

Vegetable oil spray
1½ cups (7½ ounces) all-purpose flour
1 tablespoon ground ginger
½ teaspoon baking powder
¼ teaspoon baking soda
½ teaspoon salt
¼ teaspoon ground cinnamon
1 cup packed (7 ounces) light brown sugar
¾ cup (6 ounces) water
½ cup molasses
2 large eggs
⅓ cup vegetable oil

GATHER BAKING EQUIPMENT

8-inch square metal baking pan
8-inch square piece of parchment paper (see page 146)
2 bowls (1 large, 1 medium)
Whisk
Rubber spatula
Toothpick
Oven mitts
Cooling rack
Cutting board
Chef's knife

WORK IT

1. Adjust oven rack to middle position and heat oven to 350 degrees. Spray inside bottom and sides of 8-inch square metal baking pan with vegetable oil spray. Line bottom of baking pan with 8-inch square piece of parchment paper.

2. In large bowl, whisk together flour, ginger, baking powder, baking soda, salt, and cinnamon.

3. In medium bowl, whisk brown sugar, water, molasses, eggs, and oil until smooth.

4. Add half of brown sugar mixture to flour mixture. Use rubber spatula to stir well until batter is very smooth, about 1 minute. Add remaining brown sugar mixture and stir well again until batter is completely smooth, about 1 minute.

5. Use rubber spatula to scrape batter into parchment-lined baking pan and smooth top (make sure to spread batter into corners to create even layer).

6. Place baking pan in oven. Bake until cake is deep golden brown and toothpick inserted in center comes out clean (see photo, page 15), 40 to 45 minutes.

7. Use oven mitts to remove baking pan from oven (ask an adult for help). Place baking pan on cooling rack and let cake cool completely in pan, about 1½ hours.

8. Remove cake from baking pan and discard parchment (following photos, page 147). Cut cake into pieces and serve.

Usually, when making cakes, it's important to stir the batter very gently (and not a lot!). That's because gluten, the protein in flour that turns into a network when mixed with water, becomes stronger and stronger the more you stir. Often, a super-strong gluten network means a tough cake. And nobody wants that. But this cake is different. Gingerbread batter is heavy and wet and needs a strong gluten network to make sure it doesn't sink in the middle while baking. So it's important to work your arm muscles with this recipe, stirring and stirring the batter until it's super smooth!

POUND CAKE

SERVES 12
TOTAL TIME: 1 HOUR AND 40 MINUTES, PLUS 2¼ HOURS COOLING TIME

PREPARE INGREDIENTS

Vegetable oil spray with flour
1½ cups (6 ounces) cake flour
1 teaspoon baking powder
½ teaspoon salt
16 tablespoons (2 sticks) unsalted
  butter, cut into 8 pieces
1¼ cups (8¾ ounces) sugar
4 large eggs
1½ teaspoons vanilla extract

GATHER BAKING EQUIPMENT

8½-by-4½-inch metal loaf pan
Large bowl
Whisk
Liquid measuring cup
Food processor
Rubber spatula
Toothpick
Oven mitts
Cooling rack
Butter knife
Cutting board
Chef's knife

"The directions were simple to follow. I really liked the crust on top, and it tastes good."
—Emma, 10

START BAKING! ←≪≪≪

1. Adjust oven rack to middle position and heat oven to 325 degrees. Spray inside bottom and sides of 8½-by-4½-inch metal loaf pan with vegetable oil spray with flour.

2. In large bowl, whisk together flour, baking powder, and salt. In liquid measuring cup, melt butter (see page 13 for how to melt butter).

3. Add sugar, eggs, and vanilla to food processor and lock lid into place. Turn on processor and process until well combined, about 10 seconds.

4. With processor running, slowly pour hot melted butter through feed tube until combined, about 30 seconds. Stop processor.

5. Remove lid and carefully remove processor blade (ask an adult for help). Pour butter mixture into bowl with flour mixture, making sure to scrape all butter mixture into bowl using rubber spatula.

6. Use rubber spatula to gently stir batter until just combined and no dry flour is visible. Do not overmix (see page 38). Scrape batter into greased loaf pan.

7. Place loaf pan in oven. Bake until cake is deep golden brown and toothpick inserted in center comes out with few crumbs attached (see photo, page 15), 55 minutes to 1 hour.

8. Use oven mitts to remove loaf pan from oven (ask an adult for help). Place loaf pan on cooling rack and let cake cool in pan for 15 minutes.

9. Carefully run butter knife around edges of cake to loosen from loaf pan (ask an adult for help—pan will be hot). Use oven mitts to carefully turn loaf pan on its side and remove cake from pan. Let cake cool completely on cooling rack, about 2 hours. Transfer cake to cutting board, cut, and serve.

HOW MANY POUNDS IS YOUR POUND CAKE?

Why is a pound cake called a pound cake? The earliest versions of this recipe were made in England in the 1700s and called for 1 pound each of butter, sugar, eggs, and flour. This made it easy for cooks to remember the recipe, but it also made a VERY large cake! Over the years, home cooks scaled down the recipe to make a smaller cake and added some ingredients here and there, including leaveners (such as baking powder) to make sure the cake would rise.

"The cake was just right—not too hard and not too crumbly, and the frosting was just right too—not too sweet." —Madison, 8

YELLOW SHEET CAKE WITH CHOCOLATE FROSTING

SERVES 18
TOTAL TIME: 1 HOUR AND 10 MINUTES,
  PLUS 2 HOURS COOLING TIME

PREPARE INGREDIENTS

Vegetable oil spray
2¼ cups (9 ounces) cake flour
1¼ teaspoons baking powder
¼ teaspoon baking soda
¾ teaspoon salt
4 large eggs
1¾ cups (12¼ ounces) sugar
10 tablespoons unsalted butter,
  melted and cooled (see page 13
  for how to melt butter)
5 tablespoons vegetable oil
¾ cup (6 ounces) buttermilk
2 teaspoons vanilla extract
3 cups Chocolate Frosting (page 165)

GATHER BAKING EQUIPMENT

13-by-9-inch metal baking pan
13-by-9-inch piece of parchment paper
  (see page 146)
Medium bowl
Whisk
Electric mixer (stand mixer with whisk attachment
  or handheld mixer and large bowl)
Rubber spatula
Toothpick
Oven mitts
Cooling rack
Serving platter or cutting board
Icing spatula
Chef's knife

1. Adjust oven rack to middle position and heat oven to 350 degrees. Spray inside bottom and sides of 13-by-9-inch metal baking pan with vegetable oil spray. Line bottom of baking pan with 13-by-9-inch piece of parchment paper.

2. In medium bowl, whisk together flour, baking powder, baking soda, and salt.

3. Add eggs to bowl of stand mixer (or large bowl if using handheld mixer). Lock bowl into place and attach whisk attachment to stand mixer, if using. Start mixer on medium speed. Whip eggs until foamy, 1 to 2 minutes. Stop mixer.

4. Add sugar to eggs and start mixer on medium-high speed. Whip mixture until pale yellow and fluffy, about 3 minutes.

5. Reduce speed to medium. With mixer running, very slowly pour in melted butter and oil and mix until fully combined, about 2 minutes. Stop mixer.

6. Carefully add half of flour mixture. Start mixer on low speed and mix until just combined, about 30 seconds. With mixer running, add buttermilk and vanilla and mix until combined, about 30 seconds. Stop mixer.

7. Add remaining flour mixture. Start mixer on low speed and mix until just combined and no dry flour is visible, about 30 seconds. Stop mixer. Remove bowl from stand mixer, if using.

8. Use rubber spatula to scrape down sides of bowl and stir in any remaining dry flour. Use rubber spatula to scrape batter into parchment-lined baking pan and smooth top (make sure to spread batter into corners to create even layer).

9. Place baking pan in oven. Bake until cake is golden brown and toothpick inserted in center comes out with few crumbs attached (see photo, page 15), 27 to 30 minutes.

10. Use oven mitts to remove baking pan from oven (ask an adult for help). Place baking pan on cooling rack and let cake cool completely in pan, about 2 hours. (This is a good time to make the frosting!)

11. Remove cake from baking pan and discard parchment (following photos, page 147). Use icing spatula to spread frosting evenly over top and sides of cooled cake (see photo, page 163). Cut cake into pieces and serve.

CARROT SHEET CAKE WITH CREAM CHEESE FROSTING

SERVES 18
TOTAL TIME: 1½ HOURS,
    PLUS 2 HOURS COOLING TIME

PREPARE INGREDIENTS

Vegetable oil spray
2½ cups (12½ ounces) all-purpose flour
1¼ teaspoons ground cinnamon
1¼ teaspoons baking powder
1 teaspoon baking soda
½ teaspoon salt
½ teaspoon ground nutmeg
1½ cups vegetable oil
1½ cups (10½ ounces) sugar
½ cup packed (3½ ounces) light brown sugar
4 large eggs
1 pound carrots, peeled and grated
  (see photo, right)
3 cups Cream Cheese Frosting
  (page 167)

GATHER BAKING EQUIPMENT

13-by-9-inch metal baking pan
13-by-9-inch piece of parchment paper (see page 146)
2 bowls (1 medium, 1 large)
Whisk
Rubber spatula
Toothpick
Oven mitts
Cooling rack
Serving platter or cutting board
Icing spatula
Chef's knife

1. Adjust oven rack to middle position and heat oven to 350 degrees. Spray inside bottom and sides of 13-by-9-inch metal baking pan with vegetable oil spray. Line bottom of baking pan with 13-by-9-inch piece of parchment paper.

2. In medium bowl, whisk together flour, cinnamon, baking powder, baking soda, salt, and nutmeg.

3. In large bowl, whisk oil, sugar, brown sugar, and eggs until fully combined, about 1 minute.

4. Add flour mixture to oil mixture and use rubber spatula to stir until just combined and no dry flour is visible. Add carrots to batter and stir until well combined.

5. Use rubber spatula to scrape batter into parchment-lined baking pan and smooth top (make sure to spread batter into corners to create even layer).

6. Place baking pan in oven. Bake until cake is golden brown and toothpick inserted in center comes out clean (see photo, page 15), 35 to 40 minutes.

7. Use oven mitts to remove baking pan from oven (ask an adult for help). Place baking pan on cooling rack and let cake cool completely in pan, about 2 hours. (This is a good time to make the frosting!)

8. Remove cake from baking pan and discard parchment (following photos, page 147). Use icing spatula to spread frosting evenly over top and sides of cooled cake (see photo, page 163). Cut cake into pieces and serve.

TWO WAYS TO GRATE CARROTS

There are two ways to grate carrots: with a box grater or with a food processor. If using a box grater, make sure to use the large holes on the grater and stop grating when your fingers get close to the grater. You can also use the shredding disk of a food processor to quickly and easily grate the peeled and trimmed carrots for this recipe. Be sure to ask an adult for help when removing the sharp disk!

YELLOW CUPCAKES WITH STRAWBERRY FROSTING

MAKES 12 CUPCAKES
TOTAL TIME: 1 HOUR, PLUS 1¼ HOURS COOLING TIME

PREPARE INGREDIENTS

1¾ cups (8¾ ounces) all-purpose flour
1 cup (7 ounces) sugar
1½ teaspoons baking powder
¾ teaspoon salt
12 tablespoons unsalted butter, cut
    into 12 pieces and softened (see
    page 13 for how to soften butter)
3 large eggs
¾ cup (6 ounces) milk
1½ teaspoons vanilla extract
3 cups Strawberry Frosting (page 168)

GATHER BAKING EQUIPMENT

12-cup muffin tin
12 paper cupcake liners
Electric mixer (stand mixer with paddle
    attachment or handheld mixer and
    large bowl)
Whisk
Rubber spatula
⅓-cup dry measuring cup
Toothpick
Oven mitts
Cooling rack
Small icing spatula or spoon

"The recipe was so good! I had a soccer game,
so I made an extra batch for my soccer team.
They loved it!" —Perrie, 9

START BAKING!

1. Adjust oven rack to middle position and heat oven to 350 degrees. Line 12-cup muffin tin with 12 paper liners.

2. In bowl of stand mixer (or large bowl if using handheld mixer), whisk together flour, sugar, baking powder, and salt. Lock bowl into place and attach paddle to stand mixer, if using.

3. Start mixer on low speed. Add softened butter, 1 piece at a time, and beat until mixture looks like coarse sand, about 1 minute.

4. Add eggs, one at a time, and beat until combined, about 30 seconds.

5. Add milk and vanilla, increase speed to medium, and beat until light and fluffy, about 2 minutes. Stop mixer. Remove bowl from stand mixer, if using. Use rubber spatula to scrape down sides of bowl and stir in any remaining dry flour.

6. Use ⅓-cup dry measuring cup to divide batter evenly among muffin tin cups (use rubber spatula to scrape batter from measuring cup, if needed).

7. Place muffin tin in oven. Bake cupcakes until toothpick inserted in center of 1 cupcake comes out clean (see photo, page 15), 22 to 24 minutes.

8. Use oven mitts to remove muffin tin from oven (ask an adult for help). Place muffin tin on cooling rack and let cupcakes cool in muffin tin for 15 minutes.

9. Remove cupcakes from muffin tin and transfer directly to cooling rack. Let cupcakes cool completely, about 1 hour. (This is a good time to make the frosting!)

10. Use small icing spatula or spoon to spread 2 to 3 tablespoons frosting over each cupcake (see photos, page 163). (Note you may have extra frosting. See Extra Frosting? Store It! sidebar, below, for tips on storage.) Serve.

EXTRA FROSTING? STORE IT!

Or just eat it with a spoon. (We won't tell!) But if you do want to store your extra frosting, it can be refrigerated for up to 3 days. When ready to use, let frosting soften at room temperature for 1 to 2 hours, then rewhip on medium speed until smooth, 2 to 5 minutes. Frosting can sit at room temperature for up to 2 hours before using.

CHOCOLATE CUPCAKES WITH NUTELLA FROSTING

MAKES 12 CUPCAKES
TOTAL TIME: 1 HOUR, PLUS 1¼ HOURS COOLING TIME

PREPARE INGREDIENTS

1 cup (5 ounces) all-purpose flour
½ teaspoon baking soda
¼ teaspoon salt
⅓ cup (1 ounce) Dutch-processed cocoa powder
⅓ cup (2 ounces) chocolate chips
½ cup (4 ounces) water
¾ cup (5¼ ounces) sugar
½ cup sour cream
½ cup vegetable oil
2 large eggs
1 teaspoon vanilla extract
3 cups Nutella Frosting (see page 166)

> "I LOVED it! It couldn't be more delicious. I begged my parents for more!" —Seth, 10
>
> "The recipe was fun. I thought the sour cream was weird and wanted to stop after that. My mom told me I wouldn't be able to taste the sour cream. She was right." —Brennan, 11

GATHER BAKING EQUIPMENT

12-cup muffin tin
12 paper cupcake liners
2 bowls (1 large, 1 medium)
Whisk
Liquid measuring cup
Oven mitts

Rubber spatula
⅓-cup dry measuring cup
Toothpick
Cooling rack
Small icing spatula or spoon

START BAKING! ←〰〰

1. Adjust oven rack to middle position and heat oven to 325 degrees. Line 12-cup muffin tin with 12 paper liners.

2. In medium bowl, whisk together flour, baking soda, and salt. In large bowl, combine cocoa and chocolate chips.

3. Heat water in liquid measuring cup in microwave until hot and steaming, 1 to 2 minutes. Use oven mitts to remove measuring cup from microwave. Carefully pour water over chocolate mixture and whisk until smooth.

4. Add sugar, sour cream, oil, eggs, and vanilla to bowl with chocolate mixture and whisk until combined. Add flour mixture and use rubber spatula to stir until just combined and no dry flour is visible.

5. Use ⅓-cup dry measuring cup to divide batter evenly among muffin tin cups (use rubber spatula to scrape batter from measuring cup if needed).

6. Place muffin tin in oven. Bake cupcakes until toothpick inserted in center of 1 cupcake comes out with few crumbs attached (see photo, page 15), 18 to 22 minutes.

7. Use oven mitts to remove muffin tin from oven (ask an adult for help). Place muffin tin on cooling rack and let cupcakes cool in muffin tin for 15 minutes.

8. Remove cupcakes from muffin tin and transfer directly to cooling rack. Let cupcakes cool completely, about 1 hour. (This is a good time to make the frosting!)

9. Use small icing spatula or spoon to spread 2 to 3 tablespoons frosting over each cupcake (see photos, page 163). (Note you may have extra frosting. See Extra Frosting? Store It! sidebar, page 157, for tips on storage.) Serve.

WHAT IS DUTCH-PROCESSED COCOA?

A process called Dutching, which was invented in the nineteenth century by a Dutch chemist and chocolatier named Coenraad Van Houten, raises cocoa powder's pH level, which gives the cocoa a fuller flavor and deeper color. (Scientists use a pH scale to measure how acidic or basic something is.) Dutch-processed cocoa, sometimes called alkalized or European-style cocoa, is the best choice for most baked goods. Using a natural (unalkalized) cocoa powder results in a drier cake.

CONFETTI LAYER CAKE

SERVES 16 TO 20
TOTAL TIME: 1 HOUR AND 20 MINUTES,
PLUS 1 HOUR COOLING TIME

PREPARE INGREDIENTS

Vegetable oil spray with flour
2¼ cups (9 ounces) cake flour
1¾ cups (12¼ ounces) sugar
2 teaspoons baking powder
1 teaspoon salt
1 cup (8 ounces) whole milk
6 large egg whites
   (see page 14 for how to separate eggs)
2 teaspoons vanilla extract
12 tablespoons unsalted butter, cut into
   12 pieces and softened (see page 13
   for how to soften butter)
5 cups Confetti Frosting (see page 164)
¼ cup rainbow sprinkles

GATHER BAKING EQUIPMENT

Two 9-inch round metal cake pans
Two 9-inch round pieces of parchment paper
   (see page 146)
Electric mixer (stand mixer with paddle attachment
   or handheld mixer and large bowl)
Whisk
4-cup liquid measuring cup (or medium bowl)
Rubber spatula
Toothpick
Oven mitts
Cooling rack
Serving platter or cake stand
Icing spatula
1-cup dry measuring cup
Chef's knife

START BAKING! ←〈〈〈〈

1. Adjust oven rack to middle position and heat oven to 350 degrees. Spray inside bottom and sides of each 9-inch round metal cake pan with vegetable oil spray with flour. Line bottom of each cake pan with 9-inch round piece of parchment paper.

2. In bowl of stand mixer (or large bowl if using handheld mixer), whisk together flour, sugar, baking powder, and salt. Lock bowl into place and attach paddle to stand mixer, if using.

3. In 4-cup liquid measuring cup (or medium bowl), whisk together milk, egg whites, and vanilla.

4. Start mixer on low speed. Add softened butter, 1 piece at a time, and mix until only pea-size pieces of butter remain, 1 to 2 minutes.

5. Slowly pour in milk mixture and mix until combined, about 1 minute. Increase speed to medium-high and beat until mixture is light and fluffy, 1 to 2 minutes. Stop mixer. Remove bowl from stand mixer, if using.

6. Use rubber spatula to scrape down sides of bowl and stir in any remaining dry flour. Use rubber spatula to divide batter evenly between parchment-lined cake pans and smooth tops (make sure to spread batter out to edges of each pan to create even layer).

7. Place cake pans in oven. Bake until cakes are golden brown and toothpick inserted in center of each cake comes out clean (see photo, page 15), 22 to 26 minutes.

8. Use oven mitts to remove cake pans from oven (ask an adult for help). Place cake pans on cooling rack and let cakes cool completely in pans, about 1 hour. (This is a good time to make the frosting!)

9. Remove cakes from cake pans and discard parchment (see photos, page 147).

10. Assemble and frost cake using icing spatula (following photos, page 162). Use your hand to gently pat sprinkles around bottom edge of cake (see page 170). Cut cake into wedges and serve.

FROSTING 101

The first step to decorating any cake or cupcake is to frost it. Remember, when frosting cupcakes and cakes, wait until they are completely cool. If they are warm, the butter in the frosting will melt and make a mess. Check out pages 170 to 171 for more decorating techniques.

FROSTING A LAYER CAKE

An icing spatula, a large spatula with a bend in the blade that's also called an offset spatula, is best here, but a butter knife will also work.

1. Place one cake layer on serving platter or cake stand. Use icing spatula to spread 1 cup frosting over top of cake.

2. Top with second cake layer and press down gently to set.

3. Use icing spatula to spread remaining 4 cups frosting over top and sides of cake.

4. Use icing spatula to gently smooth out bumps around sides of cake and to tidy areas where frosting on top and side merge. Then run spatula over top of cake again to smooth out any remaining bumps.

FROSTING CUPCAKES

A small icing spatula or small spoon works best for frosting cupcakes.

1. Mound 2 to 3 tablespoons frosting in center of cupcake.

2. Use icing spatula to spread frosting to edge of cupcake, leaving slight mound of frosting in center. Keep frosting off paper liner. Once frosted, cupcakes can be decorated with sprinkles or other treats (see decorating tips, page 171).

FROSTING A SHEET CAKE

A large icing spatula is the best tool for frosting sheet cakes.

1. Mound 2 cups frosting in center of cake. Then use icing spatula to spread frosting evenly to edges of cake.

2. Use remaining frosting to frost sides of cake. Use icing spatula to gently smooth out bumps around sides of cake and to tidy areas where frosting on top and side merge. Then run spatula over top of cake again to smooth out any remaining bumps.

CONFETTI FROSTING

MAKES 3 CUPS (ENOUGH FOR 12 CUPCAKES OR 1 SHEET CAKE)
TOTAL TIME: 20 MINUTES

PREPARE INGREDIENTS

20 tablespoons (2½ sticks) unsalted butter,
   cut into 20 pieces and softened (see page 13
   for how to soften butter)
2 tablespoons heavy cream
1½ teaspoons vanilla extract
⅛ teaspoon salt
2½ cups (10 ounces) confectioners' (powdered) sugar
⅓ cup rainbow sprinkles

GATHER BAKING EQUIPMENT

Electric mixer (stand mixer with paddle attachment
   or handheld mixer and large bowl)
Rubber spatula

TO MAKE 5 CUPS

(enough for a 2-layer cake)
Increase butter to 1 pound (4 sticks), increase cream to ¼ cup, increase vanilla to 1 tablespoon, increase salt to ¼ teaspoon, increase confectioners' sugar to 4 cups (16 ounces), and increase sprinkles to ¾ cup.

START BAKING!

1. In bowl of stand mixer (or large bowl if using handheld mixer), combine softened butter, cream, vanilla, and salt. Lock bowl into place and attach paddle to stand mixer, if using.

2. Start mixer on medium speed and beat until smooth, about 1 minute. Stop mixer. Use rubber spatula to scrape down sides of bowl.

3. Start mixer on low speed. Slowly add sugar, a little bit at a time, and beat until smooth, about 4 minutes.

4. Increase speed to medium-high and beat until frosting is light and fluffy, about 5 minutes. Stop mixer. Remove bowl from stand mixer, if using.

5. Add sprinkles to frosting and use rubber spatula to mix until well combined.

CHOCOLATE FROSTING

MAKES 3 CUPS (ENOUGH FOR 12 CUPCAKES OR 1 SHEET CAKE)
TOTAL TIME: 20 MINUTES

PREPARE INGREDIENTS

1⅔ cups (10 ounces) chocolate chips (bittersweet, semisweet, or milk chocolate)
20 tablespoons (2½ sticks) unsalted butter, cut into 20 pieces and softened (see page 13 for how to soften butter)
1 cup (4 ounces) confectioners' (powdered) sugar
¾ cup (2¼ ounces) Dutch-processed cocoa powder
Pinch salt
¾ teaspoon vanilla extract

GATHER BAKING EQUIPMENT

Medium microwave-safe bowl
Rubber spatula
Food processor

TO MAKE 5 CUPS

(enough for a 2-layer cake)
Increase chocolate chips to 3 cups (18 ounces), increase butter to 1 pound (4 sticks), increase confectioners' sugar to 1¾ cups (7 ounces), increase cocoa powder to 1¼ cups (3¾ ounces), increase salt to ⅛ teaspoon, and increase vanilla to 1½ teaspoons. In step 1, increase microwaving chocolate times to 1½ minutes.

START BAKING! ←—≪≪≪ • • • • •

1. Place chocolate chips in medium microwave-safe bowl. Heat in microwave at 50 percent power (see page 11) for 1 minute. Use rubber spatula to stir chocolate. Return to microwave and heat at 50 percent power until melted and smooth, about 1 minute longer. Let cool slightly, about 5 minutes.

2. Add softened butter, sugar, cocoa powder, and salt to food processor, and lock lid into place. Turn on processor and process until smooth, about 30 seconds. Stop processor.

3. Remove lid and use rubber spatula to scrape down sides. Add cooled chocolate and vanilla and lock lid back into place. Turn on processor and process until smooth, 10 to 15 seconds. Stop processor.

4. Remove lid and carefully remove processor blade (ask an adult for help).

NUTELLA FROSTING

MAKES 3 CUPS (ENOUGH FOR 12 CUPCAKES OR 1 SHEET CAKE)
TOTAL TIME: 20 MINUTES

PREPARE INGREDIENTS

16 tablespoons (2 sticks) unsalted butter, cut into 16
    pieces and softened (see page 13 for how to soften
    butter)
1 cup Nutella
¼ cup (¾ ounce) Dutch-processed cocoa powder
1 teaspoon vanilla extract
⅛ teaspoon salt
1 cup (4 ounces) confectioners' (powdered) sugar

GATHER BAKING EQUIPMENT

Electric mixer (stand mixer with paddle attachment or
    handheld mixer and large bowl)
Rubber spatula

TO MAKE 5 CUPS

(enough for a 2-layer cake)
Increase butter to 24 tablespoons
(3 sticks), increase Nutella to 1⅔ cups,
increase cocoa to 7 tablespoons
(1¼ ounces), increase vanilla to
2 teaspoons, increase salt to ¼
teaspoon, and increase confectioners' sugar to 1⅔ cups (6⅔ ounces).

START BAKING! ←〰〰

1. In bowl of stand mixer (or large bowl if using handheld mixer), combine softened butter, Nutella, cocoa, vanilla, and salt. Lock bowl into place and attach paddle to stand mixer, if using.

2. Start mixer on medium speed and beat until smooth, about 1 minute. Stop mixer. Use rubber spatula to scrape down sides of bowl.

3. Start mixer on low speed. Slowly add sugar, a little bit at a time, and beat until smooth, about 4 minutes.

4. Increase speed to medium-high and beat until frosting is light and fluffy, about 5 minutes. Stop mixer. Remove bowl from stand mixer, if using.

CREAM CHEESE FROSTING

MAKES 3 CUPS (ENOUGH FOR 12 CUPCAKES OR 1 SHEET CAKE)
TOTAL TIME: 20 MINUTES

PREPARE INGREDIENTS

12 ounces cream cheese, softened
6 tablespoons unsalted butter, cut into 6 pieces and
    softened (see page 13 for how to soften butter)
1½ tablespoons sour cream
1 teaspoon vanilla extract
⅛ teaspoon salt
1½ cups (6 ounces) confectioners' (powdered) sugar

GATHER BAKING EQUIPMENT

Electric mixer (stand mixer with paddle attachment or
    handheld mixer and large bowl)
Rubber spatula

TO MAKE 5 CUPS

(enough for a 2-layer cake)
Increase cream cheese to 1¼ pounds, increase butter to 12 tablespoons, increase sour cream to 2 tablespoons, increase vanilla to 2 teaspoons, increase salt to ¼ teaspoon, and increase confectioners' sugar to 2½ cups (10 ounces).

START BAKING!

1. In bowl of stand mixer (or large bowl if using handheld mixer), combine softened cream cheese, softened butter, sour cream, vanilla, and salt. Lock bowl into place and attach paddle to stand mixer, if using.

2. Start mixer on medium speed and beat until smooth, about 2 minutes. Stop mixer. Use rubber spatula to scrape down sides of bowl.

3. Start mixer on low speed. Slowly add sugar, a little bit at a time, and beat until smooth, about 4 minutes.

4. Increase speed to medium-high and beat until frosting is light and fluffy, about 4 minutes. Stop mixer. Remove bowl from stand mixer, if using.

STRAWBERRY FROSTING

MAKES 3 CUPS (ENOUGH FOR 12 CUPCAKES OR 1 SHEET CAKE)
TOTAL TIME: 20 MINUTES

PREPARE INGREDIENTS

1½ cups (¾ ounce) freeze-dried strawberries

12 ounces cream cheese, softened

6 tablespoons unsalted butter, cut into 6 pieces and softened (see page 13 for how to soften butter)

1½ tablespoons sour cream

1 teaspoon vanilla extract

⅛ teaspoon salt

1½ cups (6 ounces) confectioners' (powdered) sugar

GATHER BAKING EQUIPMENT

Large zipper-lock plastic bag

Rolling pin

Electric mixer (stand mixer with paddle attachment or handheld mixer and large bowl)

Rubber spatula

TO MAKE 5 CUPS

(enough for a 2-layer cake)
Increase freeze-dried strawberries to 2½ cups (1¼ ounces), increase cream cheese to 1¼ pounds, increase butter to 12 tablespoons, increase sour cream to 2 tablespoons, increase vanilla to 2 teaspoons, increase salt to ¼ teaspoon, and increase confectioners' sugar to 2½ cups (10 ounces).

1. Place strawberries in large zipper-lock plastic bag. Press out as much air as possible, then seal bag. Use rolling pin to gently pound strawberries into powder.

2. In bowl of stand mixer (or large bowl if using handheld mixer), combine softened cream cheese, softened butter, sour cream, vanilla, salt, and strawberry powder. Lock bowl into place and attach paddle to stand mixer, if using.

3. Start mixer on medium speed and beat until smooth, about 2 minutes. Stop mixer. Use rubber spatula to scrape down sides of bowl.

4. Start mixer on low speed. Slowly add sugar, a little bit at a time, and beat until smooth, about 4 minutes.

5. Increase speed to medium-high and beat until frosting is light and fluffy, about 4 minutes. Stop mixer. Remove bowl from stand mixer, if using.

FREEZE-DRIED...WHAT?

This frosting is a perfect pastel strawberry pink. And it comes from a very special ingredient. Yes, they are strawberries, but not fresh! Freeze-dried strawberries are the key to this fresh-tasting pink frosting. Freeze-dried strawberries aren't frozen, they've just had all their water removed. They aren't heated during this process, so they retain a lot of their natural fruity flavor. We like to use them in this frosting for exactly that reason—they taste great and won't make our frosting soupy! (Freeze-dried strawberries can be found at well-stocked grocery stores or online.)

DECORATING 101

Here are a few simple ideas for decorating cupcakes and a sheet cake. Don't forget to use your imagination, be creative, and have FUN!

DECORATING CAKES

Once you know how to make a smooth-frosted cake (see page 163), you have a blank canvas for some super-fun decorations. Here are some of our favorite ways to dress up our cakes.

~ ADDING TEXTURE ~

One of the simplest ways to decorate a cake is to give the frosting some texture. You can make wavy lines or a striped pattern by dragging a fork (or a cake comb) around the cake's sides or across the cake's top.

BOTTOM BORDER

This simple trick is one of the most elegant treatments, but it also camouflages any imperfections at the base of the cake. Press whole candies or nuts, one at a time, around the bottom edge of the cake. Instead of candies or nuts, you can also use fruit!

COATING THE SIDES

Coating the sides with small adornments—sprinkles, toasted coconut, chocolate shavings, crushed candies, cookies, or nuts—is an easy way to add visual appeal. Take a small amount of the ingredient in your hand and press it against the sides.

DECORATING CUPCAKES

There are so many ways to make your cupcakes look awesome—feel free to get wild! Here are two of our favorites.

SMOOTH CUPCAKE

1. Mound 2 to 3 tablespoons frosting in center of cupcake, forming thick layer. Use small icing spatula to spread frosting to edge of cupcake to create flat top. (Keep frosting off paper liners.)

2. Then use spatula to smooth frosting so it is flush with edges of cupcake. Smooth edge of frosting so it is straight up and down. Flatten top again as necessary.

3. To decorate sides of frosted cupcake: place sprinkles, chopped nuts, or crushed candy on small plate. Holding cupcake at its base, gently roll outer edge of frosting in topping.

SWIRLY CUPCAKE

Use a large open star decorating tip (see page 173) in your pastry bag.

1. Fill pastry bag with 2 different colors of frosting, one on each side of bag (see photos, page 172, for more on filling a pastry bag).

2. Starting at outside edge of cupcake and working toward center, pipe frosting into spiral shape.

3. Then stop squeezing bag and pull bag straight up and away from cupcake to ensure a neat spiral.

HOW TO FILL A PASTRY BAG

For special occasions, you may want to go all out and pipe more elaborate decorations on your cake. But before you get decorating, you'll want to be comfortable with a pastry bag. Here are the steps to filling and using one. (For information on buying a pastry bag and tips, see right.)

1. Use scissors to cut 2½ inches off bottom corner of pastry bag.

2. Fold top of pastry bag out and halfway down.

3. Insert decorating tip all the way into the bag so tip is peeking out of snipped bag corner.

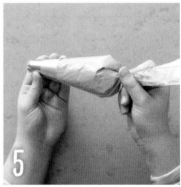

4. Stand bag upright in drinking glass (with tip touching bottom of glass). Use rubber spatula to transfer frosting to bag.

5. Twist top of bag nice and tight to push frosting down toward tip. There should be no air between frosting and top of bag.

BEGINNER'S GUIDE TO PASTRY BAGS AND TIPS

Using piping bags and tips makes piping so much easier. Here is what you will need to start piping like a professional!

Wilton disposable 16-inch pastry bag

Large open star tip

Large closed star tip

PIPING LIKE A PROFESSIONAL!

You can use your imagination when applying piping to your cakes. But for inspiration, here is one of our favorite classic decorations.

❀ ROSETTES ❀

1. Use large closed star tip and hold the bag perpendicular to surface of cake. Slowly squeeze to pipe out frosting while directing tip in tight circular motion.

2. Then stop piping and pull bag straight up and away from cake.

CAKE POPS

MAKES 24 CAKE POPS
TOTAL TIME: 1½ HOURS,
    PLUS 2¼ HOURS COOLING AND CHILLING TIME

PREPARE INGREDIENTS

Cake
Vegetable oil spray
1 cup (5 ounces) all-purpose flour
⅔ cup (4⅔ ounces) sugar
1 teaspoon baking powder
¼ teaspoon salt
6 tablespoons unsalted butter, softened
    (see page 13 for how to soften butter)
⅓ cup sour cream
1 large egg plus 1 large yolk (see page 14
    for how to separate eggs)
1 teaspoon vanilla extract

To Finish Cake Pops
3 tablespoons (1½ ounces) milk
2 cups (12 ounces) chocolate chips
    or white chocolate chips
Sprinkles or sanding sugar

"It looked store-bought and pretty because they turned out so well. The sprinkles made it look fantastic and good for valentines." —Tanner, 10½

"The recipe took a really long time to make, but when we tried them we realized they were well worth the effort. They were moist and flavorful on the inside, slightly crunchy on the outside." —Evan, 13

GATHER BAKING EQUIPMENT

8-inch round metal cake pan
8-inch round piece of parchment paper
    (see page 146)
Electric mixer (stand mixer with paddle
    attachment or handheld mixer and
    large bowl)
Whisk
Rubber spatula
Toothpick

Oven mitts
Cooling rack
1-tablespoon measuring spoon
Large plate
Plastic wrap
2-cup liquid measuring cup
24 lollipop sticks
Floral foam block (or parchment paper–lined
    baking sheet)

START BAKING! ←‹‹‹‹‹

1. **For the cake:** Adjust oven rack to middle position and heat oven to 350 degrees. Spray inside bottom and sides of 8-inch round metal cake pan with vegetable oil spray. Line bottom of cake pan with 8-inch round piece of parchment paper.

2. In bowl of stand mixer (or large bowl if using handheld mixer), whisk together flour, sugar, baking powder, and salt. Add softened butter, sour cream, egg and egg yolk, and vanilla. Lock bowl into place and attach paddle to stand mixer, if using.

3. Start mixer on medium speed and mix until batter is smooth, 1 to 2 minutes. Stop mixer. Remove bowl from stand mixer, if using.

4. Use rubber spatula to scrape down sides of bowl and stir in any remaining dry flour. Scrape batter into parchment-lined cake pan with rubber spatula and smooth top (make sure to spread batter out to edges of pan to create even layer).

5. Place cake pan in oven. Bake until cake is light golden and toothpick inserted in center comes out clean (see photo, page 15), 25 to 30 minutes.

6. Use oven mitts to remove cake pan from oven (ask an adult for help). Place cake pan on cooling rack and let cake cool completely in pan, about 1 hour.

7. Remove cake from cake pan and discard parchment (following photos, page 147). (Cooled cake can be wrapped in plastic wrap and stored at room temperature for up to 24 hours.)

KEEP GOING! »»»»→

CAKE POPS IN A HURRY!

If you need to save on time, one option is to use store-bought plain pound cake as a base for the cake pops instead of baking your own cake. Measure out 15 ounces of cake and break into 1-inch pieces (about 7 cups of 1-inch pieces), and start the recipe at step 8.

8. For the cake pops: In clean, dry bowl of stand mixer (or clean, dry large bowl if using handheld mixer), break cooled cake into rough 1-inch pieces. Add milk to bowl. Lock bowl into place and attach paddle to stand mixer, if using.

9. Start mixer on medium-low speed. Mix until cake has broken into fine crumbs and begins to clump together, 2 to 4 minutes. Stop mixer. (Mixture should feel like cookie dough when pinched together. If mixture is still crumbly, add 1 more tablespoon milk and mix until dough comes together.)

10. Use 1-tablespoon measuring spoon to scoop 1 tablespoon dough (dough should be packed into spoon). Roll dough into ball and place on large plate. Repeat with remaining dough to make 24 dough balls. Cover with plastic wrap. Place plate in freezer and freeze until firm, 45 minutes to 1 hour.

11. Place chocolate chips in 2-cup liquid measuring cup. Heat in microwave at 50 percent power (see page 11) for 1 minute. Use rubber spatula to stir chocolate. Return to microwave and heat at 50 percent power until melted and smooth, about 1 minute longer.

12. Working with 1 chilled cake ball at a time, insert lollipop stick, dip into melted chocolate, and transfer to floral foam block before decorating with sprinkles or sanding sugar (following photos, right). (Stir and rewarm chocolate in microwave as needed to keep it fluid. If cake balls become too soft, refreeze them until firm.)

13. Let cake pops sit at room temperature until coating is set, about 30 minutes. Serve. (Cake pops can be kept at room temperature for up to 4 hours or refrigerated for up to 3 days; bring to room temperature before serving.)

MAKE IT YOUR WAY

The decorating options for cake pops are endless! You can add drops of food coloring to turn melted **white chocolate chips** into different-colored coatings and mix and match **sprinkles** or **sanding sugar** in fun combinations. You can also crush up **cookies, nuts,** or **candy** and dip the coated cake pops in th██ as a topping. Let your imagination run wild!

ASSEMBLING AND DECORATING CAKE POPS

You will need a floral foam block (available at craft stores and online) to stand the cake pops upright while the coating sets. If you are unable to find one, that's okay! You can set the dipped cake pops down on a parchment paper–lined baking sheet with the stick pointing upward (note that this will give the tops a flat appearance).

1. Insert lollipop stick into cake ball, stopping at center.

2. Dip entire cake ball into melted chocolate. Turn until completely coated (tipping measuring cup to side as needed).

3. Lift cake ball out of chocolate (do not turn upright) and gently shake from side to side to allow extra coating to drip off, about 15 seconds.

4. Turn cake pop upright and gently twist back and forth to even out coating.

5. Insert stick into foam block (or stand upside down on parchment paper–lined baking sheet).

6. Sprinkle with your favorite sprinkles or sanding sugar. (Make sure to work quickly! The sprinkles will only stick to the cake pops when the chocolate is still melted.)

OLIVE OIL CAKE

SERVES 12

TOTAL TIME: 1 HOUR AND 25 MINUTES, PLUS 2¼ HOURS COOLING TIME

PREPARE INGREDIENTS

Vegetable oil spray
1¾ cups (8¾ ounces) all-purpose flour
1 teaspoon baking powder
¾ teaspoon salt
3 large eggs
¼ teaspoon grated lemon zest
   (see page 17 for how to zest citrus)
1¼ cups (8¾ ounces) plus 2 tablespoons
   sugar, measured separately
¾ cup extra-virgin olive oil
¾ cup (6 ounces) milk

GATHER BAKING EQUIPMENT

9-inch springform pan
Medium bowl
Whisk
Electric mixer (stand mixer with whisk
   attachment or handheld mixer and
   large bowl)
Rubber spatula
Toothpick
Oven mitts
Cooling rack
Spatula
Cutting board
Chef's knife

ALL ABOUT OLIVE OIL

Just about anything you bake will contain fat in some form—usually butter or vegetable oil. Fat gives baked goods flavor and a tender texture. Another kind of fat is olive oil, which is simply the juice that's pressed out of fresh olives. It's been used in cooking for thousands of years, especially in Mediterranean countries such as Italy, Greece, and Spain, where olives love to grow. Unlike butter and vegetable oil, which have mild flavors, olive oil has a strong flavor all its own—many people describe it as peppery and grassy. Because of this, you usually see olive oil only in recipes for savory foods. But you can bake with it, too! In this recipe, olive oil gives the cake a unique (and tasty) flavor and helps it bake up extra moist and tender. Make sure to use a good-quality extra-virgin olive oil in this cake.

START BAKING!

1. Adjust oven rack to middle position and heat oven to 350 degrees. Spray inside bottom and sides of 9-inch springform pan with vegetable oil spray.

2. In medium bowl, whisk together flour, baking powder, and salt.

3. Add eggs to bowl of stand mixer (or large bowl if using handheld mixer). Lock bowl into place and attach whisk attachment to stand mixer, if using. Start mixer on medium speed. Whip until eggs are foamy, 1 to 2 minutes. Stop mixer.

4. Add lemon zest and 1¼ cups sugar to eggs and start mixer on high speed. Whip until mixture is pale yellow and fluffy, about 3 minutes.

5. Reduce speed to medium. With mixer running, slowly pour in oil and mix until fully combined, about 1 minute. Stop mixer.

6. Carefully add half of flour mixture. Start mixer on low speed and mix until combined, about 1 minute. With mixer running, pour in milk and mix until combined, about 30 seconds. Stop mixer.

7. Add remaining flour mixture. Start mixer on low speed and mix until well combined, about 1 minute. Stop mixer. Remove bowl from stand mixer, if using.

8. Use rubber spatula to scrape down sides of bowl and stir in any remaining dry flour. Use rubber spatula to scrape batter into greased springform pan. Sprinkle top with remaining 2 tablespoons sugar.

9. Place springform pan in oven. Bake until cake is deep golden brown and toothpick inserted in center comes out with few crumbs attached (see page 15), 40 to 45 minutes.

10. Use oven mitts to remove springform pan from oven (ask an adult for help). Place springform pan on cooling rack and let cake cool in pan for 15 minutes.

11. Remove side of springform pan (ask an adult for help—pan will be hot). Let cake cool completely on rack, about 2 hours. Slide spatula underneath cake to loosen from pan bottom, then transfer cake to cutting board. Cut into wedges and serve.

MINI TEA CAKES WITH CITRUS GLAZE

MAKES 12 TEA CAKES
TOTAL TIME: 50 MINUTES,
    PLUS 50 MINUTES COOLING TIME

PREPARE INGREDIENTS

For the Pans
2 tablespoons sugar
2 tablespoons unsalted butter, melted and
    cooled (see page 13 for how to melt butter)

Cakes
1 cup (5 ounces) all-purpose flour
½ teaspoon salt
½ teaspoon baking powder
¼ teaspoon baking soda
6 tablespoons unsalted butter,
    cut into 6 pieces and softened,
    (see page 13 for how to soften butter)
⅔ cup (4⅔ ounces) sugar
2 large eggs
1 teaspoon vanilla extract
¼ cup (2 ounces) buttermilk

Glaze
1 cup (4 ounces) confectioners' (powdered)
    sugar
¼ teaspoon grated lemon, lime, or orange
    zest plus 2 to 3 tablespoons juice, measured
    separately (zested and squeezed from 2
    lemons, 2 limes, or 1 orange) (see page 17
    for how to zest citrus)

GATHER BAKING EQUIPMENT

3 bowls (2 small, 1 large)
Small spoon
Pastry brush
12-cup muffin tin
Whisk
Electric mixer (stand mixer with paddle
    attachment or handheld mixer and large bowl)
Rubber spatula
Large spoon
Toothpick
Oven mitts
Cooling rack

"The cakes were moist and tasty, and the glaze
was a perfect sour balance to the sweet cake.
(I used lemon.)" —Grace, 13

"The tea cakes were super, super delicious. The
recipe was on the more complex side. Loved
the sweetness with the little bit of tang. Took
to a dinner party and they were a big hit!"
—Clare, 12

START BAKING! ←‹‹‹‹‹‹

1. For the pans: Adjust oven rack to lower-middle position and heat oven to 325 degrees. In small bowl, use spoon to stir together 2 tablespoons sugar and 2 tablespoons melted butter. Use pastry brush to thoroughly paint inside of each cup of 12-cup muffin tin with butter-sugar mixture (see photo, below).

2. For the cakes: In large bowl, whisk together flour, salt, baking powder, and baking soda.

3. In bowl of stand mixer (or large bowl if using handheld mixer), combine 6 tablespoons softened butter and remaining ⅔ cup sugar. Lock bowl into place and attach paddle to stand mixer, if using.

4. Start mixer on medium-high speed and beat until mixture is pale and fluffy, 3 to 4 minutes. Stop mixer.

5. Use rubber spatula to scrape down sides of bowl. Add eggs and vanilla. Start mixer on medium speed and beat until combined, about 30 seconds. Stop mixer.

6. Carefully add half of flour mixture. Start mixer on low speed and mix until combined, about 30 seconds. With mixer running, pour in buttermilk and mix until combined, about 30 seconds. Stop mixer.

KEEP GOING! ››››→

COATING THE CUPS

Use pastry brush to thoroughly paint inside of each cup of 12-cup muffin tin with melted butter-sugar mixture.

WHAT IS A TEA CAKE?

The British define a tea cake as any light, yeast-raised sweet bun with dried fruit. The Scots say a tea cake is a chocolate-covered, marshmallow-filled cookie. American southerners will tell you that a tea cake is more like a biscuit or a cookie. At America's Test Kitchen Kids, we think a tea cake is any baked good you serve with your tea. This extra-light mini cake with citrus glaze is the perfect addition to any tea party.

7. Add remaining flour mixture. Start mixer on low speed and mix until well combined, about 30 seconds. Stop mixer. Remove bowl from stand mixer, if using.

8. Use rubber spatula to scrape down sides of bowl and stir in any remaining dry flour. Use large spoon to divide batter evenly among muffin tin cups (use rubber spatula to scrape batter from spoon if needed) and smooth tops.

9. Place muffin tin in oven. Bake until cakes are light golden brown and toothpick inserted in center of 1 cake comes out clean (see photo, page 15), about 15 minutes.

10. Use oven mitts to remove muffin tin from oven (ask an adult for help). Place muffin tin on cooling rack and let cool for 10 minutes.

11. Use oven mitts to invert muffin tin over cooling rack (ask an adult for help—muffin tin will be hot) and gently tap muffin tin cups to help cakes release. Let cakes cool completely on rack, bottom side up, about 30 minutes.

12. **For the glaze:** In second small bowl, whisk together confectioners' sugar, zest, and 2 tablespoons juice. Whisk in additional juice as needed until glaze is thick but pourable.

13. Use clean spoon to spoon glaze over top of each cooled cake, letting some drip down sides. (For easy cleanup, you can place sheet of parchment paper or paper towels under cooling rack with cakes before glazing.) Let glaze set for 10 minutes before serving.

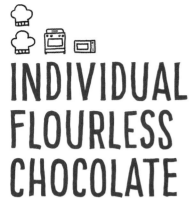

INDIVIDUAL FLOURLESS CHOCOLATE CAKES

MAKES 6 INDIVIDUAL CAKES
TOTAL TIME: 55 MINUTES,
    PLUS 2½ HOURS COOLING AND CHILLING TIME

PREPARE INGREDIENTS

Vegetable oil spray
1 cup (6 ounces) chocolate chips
8 tablespoons unsalted butter, cut into 4 pieces
½ cup (3½ ounces) sugar
1½ teaspoons cornstarch
3 large eggs
¼ cup (2 ounces) water
1½ teaspoons vanilla extract
¼ teaspoon salt

GATHER BAKING EQUIPMENT

6 (4-ounce) ramekins
Rimmed baking sheet
2 bowls (1 large microwave-safe, 1 medium)
Rubber spatula
Whisk
Large liquid measuring cup
Oven mitts
Cooling rack
Plastic wrap
Fork

NO FLOUR NEEDED FOR A FUDGY CAKE!

Flourless chocolate cakes are rich, fudgy, and intensely chocolaty. Instead of using flour or leaveners for structure, like most other cakes do, these special cakes rely on a combination of eggs and cornstarch. As the cakes bake, the eggs puff up in the oven, giving them lift. The cornstarch creates a kind of glue to keep the texture smooth. Bonus: these cakes are naturally gluten-free!

START BAKING! ←

1. Adjust oven rack to middle position and heat oven to 275 degrees. Spray inside bottoms and sides of six 4-ounce ramekins with vegetable oil spray. Place ramekins on rimmed baking sheet.

2. In large microwave-safe bowl, combine chocolate chips and butter. Heat in microwave at 50 percent power (see page 11) for 2 minutes. Stop microwave and stir mixture with rubber spatula to combine. Return to microwave and heat at 50 percent power until melted, about 2 minutes.

3. Using oven mitts, remove bowl from microwave. Use rubber spatula to stir until well combined and shiny, about 30 seconds. Let chocolate mixture cool for 5 minutes.

4. In medium bowl, whisk sugar and cornstarch until combined. Add eggs, water, vanilla, and salt and whisk until combined.

5. Add sugar mixture to cooled chocolate mixture and whisk until smooth. Use rubber spatula to transfer batter to large liquid measuring cup (make sure to scrape out all the batter!).

6. Pour batter evenly into greased ramekins (ramekins will be about three-quarters of the way full).

7. Place baking sheet in oven. Bake cakes until edges are set but centers still look wet, 20 to 24 minutes.

8. Use oven mitts to gently shake baking sheet (ask an adult for help). If centers of cakes look very liquidy and jiggle a lot, bake cakes for 1 to 2 more minutes. When centers of cakes jiggle slightly, remove baking sheet from oven (ask an adult for help). Place baking sheet on cooling rack and let cakes cool on baking sheet for 30 minutes.

9. Cover each ramekin with plastic wrap and use fork to poke small holes in top of plastic. Refrigerate until cakes are cold and firm, at least 1½ hours. (Cakes can be refrigerated for up to 2 days.)

10. Remove cakes from refrigerator and let sit at room temperature for 30 minutes before serving. Add toppings to cakes, if desired (such as Whipped Cream, page 133, berries, or dust with confectioners' sugar, page 217). Serve.

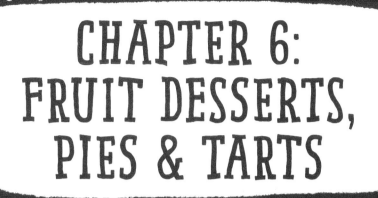

CHAPTER 6: FRUIT DESSERTS, PIES & TARTS

CRISPY, FRUITY, BISCUITY, FLAKY, CREAMY.
THESE DESSERTS ARE JUST AS IMPRESSIVE AS THEY ARE DELICIOUS.

APPLE CRISP

SERVES 8
TOTAL TIME: 1 HOUR AND 10 MINUTES,
   PLUS 30 MINUTES COOLING TIME

PREPARE INGREDIENTS

⅔ cup (3⅓ ounces) all-purpose flour
½ cup (1½ ounces) old-fashioned
   rolled oats (see page 105)
¼ cup packed (1¾ ounces)
   light brown sugar
½ teaspoon ground cinnamon
5 tablespoons unsalted butter,
   melted and cooled (see page 13
   for how to melt butter)
¼ cup (1¾ ounces) sugar
2 teaspoons cornstarch
⅛ teaspoon salt
2 pounds Golden Delicious apples, peeled,
   cored, and cut into 1-inch pieces

GATHER BAKING EQUIPMENT

2 bowls (1 large, 1 medium)
Rubber spatula
Fork
8-inch square baking dish
Oven mitts
Cooling rack

"It was so delicious. The mix of
apples and crumbles tasted like
the BEST FOOD EVER!"
—Emma, 10

SO. MANY. APPLES.

Did you know that more than 6,000 varieties of
apples are grown in North America?! They come
in different colors (red, yellow, green) and textures
(some are sweet and soft, others are tart and
crisp). When it comes to baking, we often like
to use Golden Delicious apples (as we do in this
recipe) because they are sweet and keep their
shape during baking (they don't turn into applesauce!). But you can use any sweet, crisp apple for
this recipe, such as Honeycrisp or Braeburn.

1. Adjust oven rack to lower-middle position and heat oven to 375 degrees.

2. In medium bowl, use rubber spatula to stir together flour, oats, brown sugar, and cinnamon. Drizzle melted butter over oat mixture and toss with fork or your fingers until mixture comes together (see photo, below).

3. In large bowl, use rubber spatula to stir together sugar, cornstarch, and salt. Add apples to bowl with cornstarch mixture and toss to coat.

4. Use rubber spatula to scrape apple mixture into 8-inch square baking dish. Crumble oat topping into pea-size clumps and sprinkle oat topping evenly over apple mixture.

5. Place baking dish in oven. Bake until filling is bubbling around edges and topping is golden brown, about 40 minutes.

6. Use oven mitts to remove baking dish from oven (ask an adult for help). Place baking dish on cooling rack and let apple crisp cool on rack for at least 30 minutes before serving.

MAKING A CRISP TOPPING

1. Toss oat mixture with fork or your fingers until mixture comes together.

2. Crumble oat topping into pea-size clumps and sprinkle evenly over apple mixture.

BLUEBERRY COBBLER

SERVES 8
TOTAL TIME: 1½ HOURS,
   PLUS 30 MINUTES COOLING TIME

PREPARE INGREDIENTS

Filling
1 tablespoon cornstarch
1½ teaspoons grated lemon zest plus 1
   tablespoon juice, zested and squeezed
   from 1 lemon, measured separately
Pinch salt
¾ cup (5¼ ounces) sugar
6 cups (30 ounces) blueberries

Biscuit Topping
1½ cups (7½ ounces) all-purpose flour
1½ teaspoons baking powder
½ teaspoon baking soda
½ teaspoon salt
1 tablespoon sugar
¾ cup (6 ounces) buttermilk
6 tablespoons unsalted butter, melted
   (see page 13 for how to melt butter)
Vegetable oil spray

GATHER BAKING EQUIPMENT

Rimmed baking sheet
Parchment paper
2 large bowls
Rubber spatula
8-inch square baking
   dish
Whisk
Liquid measuring cup

Fork
Oven mitts
Cooling rack
¼-cup dry
   measuring cup
Toothpick

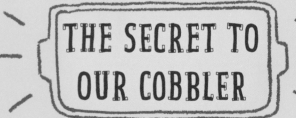

THE SECRET TO OUR COBBLER

We bake the berry filling *before* topping the cobbler with the biscuit dough. Then we bake it *again* to get our fluffy, flaky biscuits. This works so well because if the berry filling is hot when the biscuit dough is put on top, it helps cook the biscuits from the bottom while the heat from the oven cooks the top.

START BAKING! ←≪≪≪

1. **For the filling:** Adjust oven rack to middle position and heat oven to 375 degrees. Line rimmed baking sheet with parchment paper.

2. In large bowl, use rubber spatula to stir together cornstarch, lemon zest, pinch salt, and ¾ cup sugar. Add blueberries and lemon juice and gently toss to coat.

3. Use rubber spatula to scrape mixture into 8-inch square baking dish. Place baking dish on parchment-lined baking sheet. Place baking sheet in oven. Bake until filling is hot and starting to bubble around edges, about 25 minutes.

4. **For the biscuit topping:** While filling bakes, in second large bowl, whisk together flour, baking powder, baking soda, ½ teaspoon salt, and remaining 1 tablespoon sugar. In liquid measuring cup, use fork to stir buttermilk and melted butter until butter forms small clumps.

5. When filling is ready, use oven mitts to remove baking sheet from oven (ask an adult for help). Place baking sheet on cooling rack. Increase oven temperature to 475 degrees and let filling cool for 10 minutes.

6. Add buttermilk mixture to bowl with flour mixture. Use clean rubber spatula to stir until just combined.

7. Spray inside of ¼-cup dry measuring cup with vegetable oil spray. Use greased measuring cup to scoop batter and use rubber spatula to scrape off extra batter. Drop scoops of dough evenly onto warm berry filling to make 9 biscuits (see photo, below).

8. Use oven mitts to return baking dish (still on baking sheet) to oven. Bake until biscuits are golden brown and toothpick inserted in center of 1 biscuit comes out clean (see photo, page 15), 12 to 14 minutes.

9. Use oven mitts to remove baking sheet from oven (ask an adult for help). Place baking sheet on cooling rack. Let cobbler cool for at least 30 minutes before serving.

ADDING THE BISCUIT TOPPING

Spray inside of ¼-cup dry measuring cup with vegetable oil spray. Use greased measuring cup to scoop batter and use rubber spatula to scrape off extra batter. Drop scoops of dough evenly onto warm berry filling to make 9 biscuits.

S'MORES BANANA BOATS

SERVES 4
TOTAL TIME: 40 MINUTES,
   PLUS 10 MINUTES COOLING TIME

PREPARE INGREDIENTS

4 ripe bananas
½ cup (3 ounces) milk chocolate chips
¾ cup mini marshmallows
2 graham crackers, broken into small pieces

GATHER BAKING EQUIPMENT

Paring knife
Aluminum foil
Ruler
8-inch square baking dish
Oven mitts
Cooling rack

MARSHMALLOWS

BAKED BANANAS?!

The inspiration for this easy, crowd-pleasing dessert came from cooking over campfires! As Girl and Boy Scouts, we used to open bananas, add chocolate and marshmallows, wrap them completely in foil, and throw them into a fire to cook. Those S'mores Banana Boats were a little messier and not quite as pretty as ours today, but they were just as delicious. These bananas are roasted until they're just soft and scoopable, the chocolate is melted, and the marshmallows are toasty. The graham cracker crumbs give them a nice little crunch!

START BAKING! ←≪≪≪

1. Adjust oven rack to middle position and heat oven to 375 degrees.

2. Using tip of paring knife, slice bananas open lengthwise (the long way), open bananas, and wrap in foil (following photos, below).

3. Sprinkle chocolate chips evenly inside bananas, then sprinkle marshmallows on top of chocolate chips. Transfer assembled banana boats to 8-inch square baking dish.

4. Place baking dish in oven. Bake until marshmallows are golden brown and chocolate chips have melted, 12 to 15 minutes.

5. Use oven mitts to remove baking dish from oven (ask an adult for help). Place baking dish on cooling rack and let bananas cool for 10 minutes. Sprinkle bananas with graham cracker pieces. Serve.

ASSEMBLING BANANA BOATS

1. Using tip of paring knife, slice bananas open from tip to tip, leaving peels on and making sure not to slice all the way through bananas.

2. Gently push end of each banana down and toward center to open up banana into canoe shape.

3. Place four 8-by-12-inch rectangles of aluminum foil on counter. Wrap each banana peel in foil by folding up sides of foil and pinching ends together to create canoe shape.

PIE DOUGH

MAKES ONE 9-INCH SINGLE CRUST
TOTAL TIME: 15 MINUTES,
    PLUS 2 HOURS CHILLING TIME

PREPARE INGREDIENTS

1½ cups (7½ ounces) all-purpose flour
1 tablespoon sugar
½ teaspoon salt
12 tablespoons unsalted butter, cut into
    12 pieces and chilled
6 tablespoons (3 ounces) ice water (see
    page 11 for how to measure ice water)

GATHER BAKING EQUIPMENT

Food processor
Plastic wrap
Rubber spatula
Ruler

GATHER ADDITIONAL EQUIPMENT FOR SHAPING AND BAKING PIE SHELL

Rolling pin
9-inch pie plate
Kitchen shears
Fork
Plastic wrap
Aluminum foil
Pie weights (or dried beans, raw rice, or sugar)
Baking sheet
2 cooling racks

START BAKING! ←‹‹‹‹‹‹

1. Place flour, sugar, and salt in food processor. Lock lid into place. Turn on processor and process mixture for 3 seconds. Stop processor.

2. Remove lid and sprinkle chilled butter pieces over flour mixture. Lock lid back into place. Hold down pulse button for 1 second, then release. Repeat until mixture looks like coarse crumbs, about eight 1-second pulses.

3. Remove lid and pour ice water over mixture. Lock lid back into place. Turn on processor and process until little balls of butter form and almost no dry flour remains, about 10 seconds. Stop processor.

4. Remove lid and carefully remove processor blade (ask an adult for help), and form and shape dough into 6-inch disk (following photos, below).

5. Refrigerate disk of dough for at least 2 hours or up to 2 days before using, unless making Pumpkin Pie. (If making Pumpkin Pie [page 204], immediately roll out dough, fit into pie plate, and blind-bake, following photos, pages 196, 197, and 198.)

MAKING PIE DOUGH

1. Remove lid and carefully remove processor blade (ask an adult for help).

2. Lay long piece of plastic wrap on clean counter. Use rubber spatula to transfer dough to center of plastic. Gather edges of plastic together to form bundle of dough.

3. Keeping dough crumbs inside plastic, press dough crumbs together to form ball.

4. Flatten plastic-covered ball into 6-inch circle, smoothing out any cracked edges.

HOW TO USE PIE DOUGH 101

One of the best things about pie is the crust. You can make your own (page 194) or buy it from the store. Follow these steps to get your flaky, buttery goodness looking ready for pie!

ROLLING HOMEMADE PIE DOUGH

1. Sprinkle flour over clean counter. Unwrap pie dough and discard plastic wrap. Place dough on floured counter and sprinkle dough with a little extra flour. Use rolling pin to roll dough out from center.

2. Turn dough a quarter turn and continue to roll out to 12-inch circle (or as big as specified in recipe), rotating dough and reflouring counter in between rolls.

YES, YOU CAN USE STORE-BOUGHT

While homemade pie dough will always have the best texture and flavor, store-bought dough can still be very good! And it works for almost every pie-dough-related recipe in this book (all except our Free-Form Summer Fruit Tart, page 200). Our favorite store-bought dough, **Pillsbury Refrigerated Pie Crusts ($3.99 for 2 crusts)**, is simple to unfurl, fits in our pie plates without extra rolling, and bakes up golden and flaky. Though we still prefer homemade, when we don't have the time, we'll be reaching for Pillsbury.

SHAPING A PIE SHELL

1. Place rolling pin on bottom edge of dough, then loosely roll pie dough around rolling pin. Hold rolling pin over 9-inch pie plate and gently unroll dough, letting extra dough hang over edges of plate.

2. Use one hand to gently lift edge of dough and use your other hand to gently press middle of dough into bottom of pie plate. Repeat all the way around dough until dough is pressed into bottom and against sides of pie plate.

3. Use kitchen shears to trim edge of pie dough to about ½ inch beyond edge of pie plate.

4. Use your fingers to fold extra dough under itself onto rim of pie plate.

5. Use your fingers and knuckles to crimp edges of dough.

6. Use fork to prick bottom and sides of shaped pie shell all over, about 40 times. Wrap dough-lined pie plate loosely in plastic wrap. Refrigerate until dough is very firm, at least 2 hours or up to 2 days.

BLIND-BAKING PIE CRUST

Sometimes pie fillings don't need any baking (see Pumpkin Pie, page 204), but the pie crust still does. Baking a pie crust without any filling is what the experts call blind-baking. You will need 1 recipe Pie Dough (page 194), rolled out (page 196), shaped into a pie shell (page 197), and chilled—or 1 round store-bought dough, shaped into a pie shell and chilled.

1. Adjust oven rack to lowest position and heat oven to 375 degrees. Remove pie shell from refrigerator and discard plastic wrap. Cover pie shell with large sheet of aluminum foil and gently press foil against bottom and sides of dough, keeping edges covered. Fill foil-lined pie shell with pie weights (or dried beans, raw rice, or sugar).

2. Line rimmed baking sheet with aluminum foil. Place cooling rack in baking sheet. Place pie shell on baking sheet, place in oven, and bake for 45 minutes. Use oven mitts to remove baking sheet from oven (ask an adult for help) and place on second cooling rack. (Move slowly so pie plate doesn't slide!) Ask an adult to remove foil and pie weights (pie weights will be VERY hot). Crust will be pale golden brown.

3. Return baking sheet to oven and continue to bake until edges of pie crust are golden brown, 20 to 25 minutes. Use oven mitts to remove baking sheet from oven (ask an adult for help), place on second cooling rack, and let pie shell cool completely, about 1 hour.

FREE-FORM SUMMER FRUIT TART

SERVES 8
TOTAL TIME: 1 HOUR AND 20 MINUTES, PLUS 30 MINUTES COOLING TIME
   (PLUS TIME TO MAKE PIE DOUGH)

PREPARE INGREDIENTS

1 recipe Pie Dough (see page 194)
Vegetable oil spray
1 teaspoon cornstarch
¼ cup (1¾ ounces) plus 1 tablespoon
   sugar, measured separately
1 pound peaches, pitted and cut into
   ½-inch wedges (see photos, right)
1 cup (5 ounces) blackberries
All-purpose flour (for sprinkling
   on counter)
1 tablespoon (½ ounce) water

GATHER BAKING EQUIPMENT

Rimmed baking sheet
Parchment paper
Large bowl
Whisk
Rubber spatula
Rolling pin
Ruler
Pastry brush
Oven mitts
Cooling rack
Large spatula
Cutting board
Chef's knife

"I was really excited to make dough from scratch.
It was kind of hard for me to slice the fruit at first,
but then I got better." —Sophia, 8

1. Adjust oven rack to lower-middle position and heat oven to 375 degrees. Line rimmed baking sheet with parchment paper and lightly spray with vegetable oil spray.

2. In large bowl, whisk cornstarch and ¼ cup sugar until well combined. Add peaches and blackberries. Use rubber spatula to gently stir until fruit is coated with sugar mixture.

3. Sprinkle a little flour over clean counter. Place dough on floured counter and sprinkle dough with a little extra flour. Use rolling pin to roll dough into 12-inch circle, rotating dough and reflouring counter in between rolls (see photos, page 196).

4. Use your hands to gently transfer dough to parchment-lined baking sheet. Use rubber spatula to scrape fruit mixture into center of dough. Spread into even layer, leaving 2-inch border around edges.

KEEP GOING! ⇉→

PITTING AND SLICING PEACHES

1. Cut small slice off bottom of peach to create flat surface.

2. Slice around pit to remove 4 large pieces. Discard pit.

3. Cut large pieces into wedges that are roughly ½ inch thick.

5. Fold 2-inch border of dough up and over edge of filling (see photos, right). Continue folding, overlapping folds of dough every 2 inches, until you get all the way around tart.

6. Use pastry brush to lightly paint dough with water. Sprinkle dough and fruit with remaining 1 tablespoon sugar.

7. Place baking sheet in oven and bake until dough is golden brown and fruit is bubbling, 45 to 50 minutes.

8. Use oven mitts to remove baking sheet from oven (ask an adult for help). Place baking sheet on cooling rack. Let tart cool on baking sheet for 30 minutes.

9. Use large spatula to transfer tart to cutting board (ask an adult for help). Slice into wedges and serve warm or at room temperature.

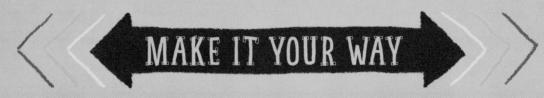

MAKE IT YOUR WAY

This tart is a great way to show off ripe summer fruit—and you don't have to stick to peaches and blackberries. You can use whatever combo of stone fruit (any fruit with a pit) and berries you can find at the grocery store or farmers' market. Swap the peaches for **plums, nectarines**, or **apricots** and the blackberries for **blueberries, raspberries**, or **strawberries**. If you can't find fresh stone fruit, you can also use 14 ounces of frozen sliced peaches, thawed and patted dry with paper towels. Try out a few different combinations to find your favorite!

Because ripe fruit is so juicy, **we don't recommend using store-bought pie dough for this recipe**, as it's too thin and delicate to hold the filling.

SHAPING A FREE-FORM TART (OR GALETTE)

1. Fold 2-inch border of dough up and over edge of filling.

2. Continue folding, overlapping folds of dough every 2 inches.

3. Use pastry brush to lightly paint dough with water (or beaten egg).

TESTING ROLLING PINS FOR KIDS

We wanted to find a good rolling pin that kids found comfortable (not too big or heavy)! We purchased six rolling pins in various styles and materials. Two were designed specifically for kids; the rest were marketed for adults but were light and small. Our kid testers gravitated toward two models that had comfortable handles, rolled smoothly over dough, and had either a long rolling surface or a wide circumference. The **Mrs. Anderson's Beechwood Rolling Pin ($19.99)** ultimately came out on top. It had a slightly longer rolling surface and was significantly heavier (though still lighter than our adult favorite), so kids could roll out dough quickly and easily. With this rolling pin, you too can be a confident pie-dough roller at home!

PUMPKIN PIE

SERVES 10
TOTAL TIME: 40 MINUTES,
PLUS 4 HOURS CHILLING TIME
(PLUS TIME TO MAKE AND BAKE PIE SHELL)

PREPARE INGREDIENTS

1 recipe Pie Dough (see page 194 to make
    your own, or use 1 round store-bought),
    rolled, shaped, blind-baked, and cooled
    (see page 198)
1 cup (8 ounces) heavy cream
1 tablespoon unflavored gelatin
1 (15-ounce) can unsweetened pumpkin
    puree, opened
¾ cup (5¼ ounces) sugar
¼ cup maple syrup
1 teaspoon salt
½ teaspoon ground cinnamon
¼ teaspoon ground nutmeg
¼ teaspoon ground ginger
Vegetable oil spray

GATHER BAKING EQUIPMENT

2 bowls (1 large microwave-safe,
    1 medium microwave-safe)
Whisk
Oven mitts
Rubber spatula
Plastic wrap
Chef's knife

"The pumpkin flavor really shined."
—Suriya, 10

START BAKING!

1. In medium microwave-safe bowl, whisk cream and gelatin until all gelatin looks wet (mixture will be slightly lumpy). Let mixture sit for 5 minutes.

2. Heat gelatin mixture in microwave for 1 minute. Use oven mitts to remove bowl from microwave and whisk until smooth and syrupy. Set aside.

3. In large microwave-safe bowl, whisk pumpkin, sugar, maple syrup, salt, cinnamon, nutmeg, and ginger until combined. Heat pumpkin mixture in microwave until steaming, about 2 minutes.

4. Use oven mitts to remove bowl from microwave. Add gelatin mixture to pumpkin mixture and carefully whisk until well combined (ask an adult for help—bowl will be HOT).

5. Use rubber spatula to scrape filling into cooled pie crust. Gently shake pie so filling spreads evenly to edges. Let pie cool for 10 minutes.

6. Lightly spray sheet of plastic wrap with vegetable oil spray. Gently press greased plastic onto filling. Refrigerate pie for at least 4 hours or up to 2 days. Slice pie into wedges and serve.

EASY AS PUMPKIN PIE

Most pumpkin pies—like the ones on your Thanksgiving table every year—have fillings that contain pumpkin puree, cream, sugar, spices, and eggs. Because of the eggs, which make the filling nice and thick, these pies need to be baked, often for a long time. In our pumpkin pie, however, we don't use eggs. Instead, we use gelatin—the same ingredient that is in Jell-O!

And instead of baking our pie, after heating up the gelatin and the pumpkin in the microwave, we chill it. (Well, we still bake the crust—called blind-baking [see page 198]—but we chill the baked crust and its nonbaked filling.)

What?! This is because gelatin is a kind of protein. It's made up of long, thin molecules. When gelatin is mixed with a hot liquid, its molecules are loose and flexible and they move around a lot—the liquid stays liquid. But when the temperature gets colder, the gelatin molecules slow down and start to get tangled, kind of like earbuds when they're in your pocket. Eventually, they get so tangled that they trap the liquid inside. The liquid can't move around or flow: it becomes a solid—in this case, a smooth, sliceable, solid pumpkin pie filling!

LEMON-OLIVE OIL TART

SERVES 10
TOTAL TIME: 1½ HOURS, PLUS 2 HOURS COOLING TIME

PREPARE INGREDIENTS

Crust
1½ cups (7½ ounces) all-purpose flour
5 tablespoons (2¼ ounces) sugar
½ teaspoon salt
2 tablespoons (1 ounce) water
½ cup extra-virgin olive oil

Filling
1 cup (7 ounces) sugar
2 tablespoons all-purpose flour
¼ teaspoon salt
3 large eggs plus 3 large yolks
1 tablespoon grated lemon zest plus
   ½ cup juice, zested and squeezed
   from 3 lemons
¼ cup extra-virgin olive oil

GATHER BAKING EQUIPMENT

2 bowls (1 large, 1 medium)
Whisk
Rubber spatula
9-inch round tart pan with removable
   bottom
Rimmed baking sheet
Oven mitts
Cooling rack
Medium saucepan
Instant-read thermometer
Fine-mesh strainer
Chef's knife

"The texture was smooth with crunch of crust in every bite." —Jacob, 12

START BAKING! ←≪≪≪

1. **For the crust:** Adjust oven rack to middle position and heat oven to 350 degrees. In medium bowl, whisk together 1½ cups flour, 5 tablespoons sugar, and ½ teaspoon salt. Add water and ½ cup oil and use rubber spatula to stir until uniform dough forms and no dry flour is visible.

2. Shape dough into 9-inch tart pan with removable bottom (following photos, below).

3. Place tart pan on rimmed baking sheet and place baking sheet in oven. Bake until crust is golden brown and firm to touch, 30 to 35 minutes.

4. Use oven mitts to remove baking sheet from oven (ask an adult for help). Place baking sheet on cooling rack.

KEEP GOING! ≫≫≫→

NO ROLLING THIS DOUGH

1. Crumble three-quarters of dough over bottom of tart pan and press to even thickness.

2. Crumble remaining one-quarter of dough evenly around edge of pan and press into sides.

3. Press dough across bottom of pan until even and smooth.

5. **For the filling**: In medium saucepan, whisk together remaining 1 cup sugar, 2 tablespoons flour, and ¼ teaspoon salt. Add eggs and egg yolks and whisk until no streaks of eggs remain. Add lemon zest and juice and whisk until combined.

6. Place saucepan over medium-low heat and cook until mixture registers 160 degrees on instant-read thermometer, 5 to 8 minutes (following photos, below). Turn off heat, slowly whisk in oil, then strain mixture through fine-mesh strainer set over large bowl. Pour strained lemon mixture into warm tart crust.

7. Place baking sheet in oven. Bake tart until filling is set and barely jiggles when tart pan is shaken (ask an adult for help), 8 to 12 minutes.

8. Use oven mitts to remove baking sheet from oven (ask an adult for help). Place baking sheet on cooling rack and let tart cool completely in tart pan, at least 2 hours.

9. Remove outer metal ring of tart pan (see photo, right). Slice tart into wedges and serve.

MAKING LEMON FILLING

1. Place saucepan over medium-low heat. Cook, whisking constantly and making sure to scrape corners of saucepan, until mixture thickens slightly and registers 160 degrees, 5 to 8 minutes.

2. Turn off heat and slide saucepan to cool burner. Slowly pour in oil and whisk until combined.

3. Set fine-mesh strainer over large bowl. Pour lemon mixture through strainer, pressing on mixture with clean rubber spatula (ask an adult for help if saucepan is heavy!).

REMOVING THE SIDES OF A TART PAN

To remove outer metal ring of pan, place one hand under bottom of cooled tart pan and lift up off cooling rack. As you lift up, outer metal ring will drop down onto your arm.

COOKIES AND CREAM ICE CREAM PIE

SERVES 12
TOTAL TIME: 50 MINUTES, PLUS 30 MINUTES
 COOLING TIME, PLUS 3 HOURS CHILLING TIME

PREPARE INGREDIENTS

Crust
Vegetable oil spray
16 Oreo cookies, broken into large pieces
2 tablespoons unsalted butter, melted (see
   page 13 for how to melt butter)

Filling
2 pints cookies and cream ice cream
8 Oreo cookies, broken into large pieces
2 cups Whipped Cream (page 133)
   (optional)

GATHER BAKING EQUIPMENT

9-inch pie plate
Food processor
Rubber spatula
Oven mitts
Cooling rack
Large bowl
Large spoon
Plastic wrap
Chef's knife

"I liked it because it was fun to
mash the cookies and put them
into the pie pan and then into
the ice cream." —Jack, 8

START BAKING!

1. **For the crust:** Adjust oven rack to middle position and heat oven to 325 degrees. Spray 9-inch pie plate with vegetable oil spray.

2. Add 16 Oreo cookies (broken into large pieces) to food processor and lock lid into place. Hold down pulse button for 1 second, then release. Repeat until cookies are coarsely ground, about fifteen 1-second pulses.

3. Turn on processor and process until crumbs are uniformly fine, about 15 seconds. Stop processor and remove lid. Add melted butter to processor and lock lid back into place. Turn on processor and process until mixture resembles wet sand, about 15 seconds.

4. Stop processor, remove lid, and carefully remove processor blade (ask an adult for help). Use rubber spatula to scrape mixture into greased pie plate. Use your hands to press crumbs into even layer covering bottom and sides of pie plate.

5. Place pie plate in oven and bake for 15 minutes.

6. Use oven mitts to remove pie plate from oven (ask an adult for help). Place pie plate on cooling rack and let crust cool completely, about 30 minutes.

7. **For the filling:** Remove ice cream from freezer and let soften on counter for 10 to 15 minutes. In large bowl, combine softened ice cream and remaining 8 Oreo cookies (broken into large pieces). Use back of large spoon to mash until well combined.

8. Use rubber spatula to transfer ice cream mixture to cooled crust and smooth top. Cover pie with plastic wrap and freeze until filling is completely frozen, at least 3 hours or up to 1 week.

9. Slice pie into wedges. Dollop each piece of pie with Whipped Cream (if using). Serve.

↓ ↓ ↓ MAKE IT YOUR WAY ↓ ↓ ↓

Once you master the basics of ice cream pies, you can really go wild creating your own flavor variations. Lots of other cookies can be substituted for the Oreo cookies, such as **animal crackers** or **peanut butter sandwich cookies**. Plus, you can use any flavor of **ice cream** you want—**vanilla, chocolate, mint chocolate chip.** You can also add toppings such as **sprinkles, Reese's Pieces candy**, or **M&M's candies.** The possibilities are endless. Get creative and have fun mixing and matching!

RUFFLED MILK PIE

SERVES 8
TOTAL TIME: 1¼ HOURS, PLUS 30 MINUTES COOLING TIME

PREPARE INGREDIENTS

10 to 12 (14-by-9-inch) phyllo sheets,
    thawed in refrigerator overnight or
    on counter for 4 to 5 hours (do not
    use microwave)
6 tablespoons unsalted butter,
    melted and cooled (see page 13
    for how to melt butter)
1½ cups (12 ounces) whole milk
3 large eggs
½ cup (3½ ounces) sugar
1 teaspoon vanilla extract
¼ teaspoon ground cinnamon
¼ teaspoon salt
1 to 2 teaspoons confectioners'
    (powdered) sugar, for dusting

GATHER BAKING EQUIPMENT

Rimmed baking sheet
Plastic wrap
Clean dish towel
Pastry brush
9-inch round metal cake pan
2 bowls (1 medium, 1 small)
Whisk
Oven mitts
Cooling rack
Fine-mesh strainer
Chef's knife

"I felt like I was making art." —Beatrix, 10

START BAKING!

1. Adjust oven rack to middle position and heat oven to 350 degrees. Place phyllo sheets on rimmed baking sheet. Cover with large sheet of plastic wrap. Sprinkle clean dish towel with water until just damp. Place damp towel on top of plastic.

2. Use pastry brush to paint inside of 9-inch round metal cake pan lightly with a little bit of melted butter.

3. Remove 1 phyllo sheet from stack (keeping remaining sheets covered) and place on clean counter with long side facing you.

KEEP GOING! ⇶→

HELLO, PHYLLO

Phyllo ("FEE-low") is a paper-thin dough made from flour, water, and a little bit of oil. It's rolled out into sheets that look like tissue paper and is found in the frozen section of the grocery store. Phyllo is a popular ingredient in Greek cooking, and the layers of dough, brushed with butter or oil, make crackly, flaky crusts for dishes such as baklava (a pastry made with nuts and honey) or spanakopita (a spinach-and-cheese pie). Phyllo is also used in this Ruffled Milk Pie (also called *galaktoboureko*, a Greek custard pie that's often served at Easter), where the edges of the sheets make a pretty ruffled pattern! When working with frozen phyllo, don't thaw the phyllo in the microwave; let it sit in the refrigerator overnight or on the counter for 4 to 5 hours before using it.

4. Use pastry brush to paint phyllo with melted butter, then shape into ruffled spiral (following photos, right). Continue to brush each phyllo sheet with butter, scrunch into strip, and add to cake pan until pan is full.

5. Place cake pan in oven and bake until phyllo is golden brown, 30 to 35 minutes. (This recipe was developed using a light-colored cake pan. If using a dark-colored cake pan, reduce baking time to 20 to 25 minutes.)

6. While phyllo bakes, in medium bowl, whisk milk, eggs, sugar, vanilla, cinnamon, and salt until well combined.

7. When phyllo is ready, use oven mitts to remove cake pan from oven (ask an adult for help). Place cake pan on cooling rack. Pour milk mixture evenly over phyllo in cake pan.

8. Use oven mitts to return cake pan to oven and bake until filling is set and no longer jiggles when pan is gently shaken (ask an adult for help), 20 to 24 minutes.

9. Use oven mitts to remove cake pan from oven (ask an adult for help). Place cake pan on cooling rack and let pie cool on rack for 30 minutes.

10. Dust pie with confectioners' sugar (following photos, page 217). Slice pie into wedges and serve warm.

MAKING RUFFLED MILK PIE

1. Use pastry brush to paint phyllo lightly with melted butter. (Don't worry if the phyllo breaks or tears—it's OK!)

2. Use your hands to push short sides of phyllo sheet toward one another, scrunching into loose accordion-shaped strip.

3. Starting at one end, roll strip into spiral shape. Place in center of greased cake pan. Note that you will only spiral first phyllo. Following phyllo strips will go around first spiral.

4. Repeat steps 1 and 2 and continue to place phyllo strips in cake pan until pan is filled with large spiral shape.

RASPBERRY CLAFOUTI

SERVES 8
TOTAL TIME: 35 MINUTES, PLUS 30 MINUTES COOLING TIME

PREPARE INGREDIENTS

1 tablespoon unsalted butter, softened
   (see page 13 for how to soften butter)
2 large eggs
⅓ cup (2⅓ ounces) sugar
1¼ teaspoons vanilla extract
⅛ teaspoon salt
¼ cup (1¼ ounces) all-purpose flour
½ cup (4 ounces) heavy cream
⅓ cup (2⅔ ounces) whole milk
1½ cups (7½ ounces) raspberries
1 to 2 teaspoons confectioners' (powdered)
   sugar, for dusting

GATHER BAKING EQUIPMENT

9-inch pie plate
Rimmed baking sheet
2 bowls (1 large, 1 small)
Whisk
Oven mitts
Cooling rack
Fine-mesh strainer
Chef's knife

"My sister was licking the plate clean it was so good!" —Avery, 10

WHERE PANCAKES MEET CUSTARD

This custardy dessert comes from France, where the verb *clafir* means "to fill." In other words, clafouti is a dessert *filled* with fruit. The batter is made from eggs, cream, and flour. Because a clafouti is basically a combination of a custard and a pancake, it's important for it not to have too much flour (it would be too pancake-y) or too many eggs or too much cream (too custardy). Ours strikes a nice balance between the two, especially when studded with fruit. Clafoutis are traditionally made with cherries; we chose raspberries because they're easy to find year-round, but you can experiment with whatever seasonal fruit you find!

1. Adjust oven rack to lower-middle position and heat oven to 425 degrees. Use your fingers to grease 9-inch pie plate with softened butter. Place pie plate on rimmed baking sheet.

2. In large bowl, whisk eggs, sugar, vanilla, and salt until smooth and pale, about 1 minute. Add flour and whisk until smooth, about 30 seconds.

3. Add cream and milk and whisk until combined.

4. Pour batter into greased pie plate. Sprinkle raspberries evenly over top.

5. Place baking sheet in oven. Bake clafouti until it puffs above edges of pie plate and turns golden brown (edges will be dark brown), 16 to 20 minutes.

6. Use oven mitts to remove baking sheet from oven (ask an adult for help). Place baking sheet on cooling rack and let clafouti cool for 30 minutes.

7. Dust clafouti with confectioners' sugar (following photos, right). Slice into wedges and serve.

DUSTING CONFECTIONERS SUGAR ON DESSERTS

1. Set fine-mesh strainer over small b Add confectioners' sugar to straine

2. Use fine-mesh strainer to dust co tioners' sugar evenly over baked g gently tapping sides of straine release sugar.

CONVERSIONS & EQUIVALENTS

The recipes in this book were developed using standard U.S. measures. The charts below offer equivalents for U.S. and metric measures. All conversions are approximate and have been rounded up or down to the nearest whole number.

VOLUME CONVERSIONS

U.S.	METRIC
1 teaspoon	5 milliliters
2 teaspoons	10 milliliters
1 tablespoon	15 milliliters
2 tablespoons	30 milliliters
¼ cup	59 milliliters
⅓ cup	79 milliliters
½ cup	118 milliliters
¾ cup	177 milliliters
1 cup	237 milliliters
2 cups (1 pint)	473 milliliters
4 cups (1 quart)	0.946 liter
4 quarts (1 gallon)	3.8 liters

WEIGHT CONVERSIONS

OUNCES	GRAMS
½	14
¾	21
1	28
2	57
3	85
4	113
5	142
6	170
8	227
10	283
12	340
16 (1 pound)	454

OVEN TEMPERATURES

FAHRENHEIT	CELSIUS	GAS MARK
225	105	¼
250	120	½
275	135	1
300	150	2
325	165	3
350	180	4
375	190	5
400	200	6
425	220	7
450	230	8
475	245	9

CONVERTING TEMPERATURES FROM AN INSTANT-READ THERMOMETER

We include doneness temperatures in some recipes in this book. We recommend an instant-read thermometer for the job. To convert Fahrenheit degrees to Celsius:

Subtract 32 degrees from the Fahrenheit reading, then divide the result by 1.8.

Example
"Roast chicken until thighs register 175°F degrees"

To Convert
175°F − 32 = 143°
143° ÷ 1.8 = 79.44°C, rounded down to 79°C

RECIPE STATS

PER SERVING		CALORIES	FAT (G)	SATURATED FAT (G)	SODIUM (MG)	CARBOHYDRATES (G)	FIBER (G)	TOTAL SUGAR (G)	ADDED SUGAR (G)	PROTEIN (G)
MUFFINS, QUICK BREADS & OTHER BREAKFAST TREATS										
Spiced Applesauce Muffins	per muffin	190	8	5	200	28	1	14	11	3
Banana and Chocolate Chip Mini Muffins	per muffin	90	3	1.5	55	14	0	7	5	1
Whole-Wheat Raspberry Muffins	per muffin	320	11	3.5	380	51	6	21	19	7
Corn Muffins	per muffin	240	11	6	270	31	1	9	8	5
Zucchini Bread	serves 10	240	7	1	420	41	2	23	21	5
Pumpkin Bread with Chocolate Chips	serves 10	310	16	3.5	240	41	1	29	28	4
Quick Cheese Bread	serves 10	260	13	8	540	23	0	2	0	12
Simple Cream Scones	per scone	280	18	11	320	27	0	6	5	4
Berry Scones	per scone	190	9	6	240	23	1	6	4	3
Crumb Cake	serves 16	250	10	6	85	36	1	15	15	3
Mini Muffin Tin Doughnut Holes	per doughnut	90	4	2.5	85	12	0	7	6	1
Popovers	per popover	190	5	3	280	26	1	3	0	8
Buttermilk Biscuits	per biscuit	150	6	3.5	390	20	0	3	1	4
Cherry, Almond, Chocolate Chip Granola	per ½ cup	310	15	3	65	41	4	18	11	6
YEAST BREADS										
Easy Whole-Wheat Sandwich Bread	per ¾-inch slice	140	2.5	1.5	200	25	3	1	1	5
Almost No-Knead Bread	serves 10	150	0	0	470	31	0	0	0	4
Roman-Style Focaccia	serves 8	220	7	1	350	33	0	1	1	5
Middle Eastern Za'atar Bread	serves 12	220	9	1.5	390	27	1	1	1	5
Fluffy Dinner Rolls	per roll	200	7	4	280	29	0	5	4	5
Cinnamon Rolls	per roll	300	9	5	270	49	0	25	25	4
Soft Pretzels	per pretzel	270	8	3.5	560	41	1	2	2	7

	PER SERVING	CALORIES	FAT (G)	SATURATED FAT (G)	SODIUM (MG)	CARBOHYDRATES (G)	FIBER (G)	TOTAL SUGAR (G)	ADDED SUGAR (G)	PROTEIN (G)
PIZZA, FLATBREAD & OTHER SAVORY BAKED GOODS										
Personal Pizzas	per pizza	380	14	6	1130	45	2	3	1	17
Easy Pizza Sauce	per 2 tablespoons	25	2	0	150	2	0	1	0	0
Tear-and-Share Pepperoni Pizza Rolls	per roll	170	8	3	490	16	1	1	0	7
Buffalo Chicken Lavash Flatbread	serves 4	250	14	6	430	11	0	1	0	18
Corn, Tomato, and Bacon Galette	serves 8	370	25	14	410	26	0	3	2	9
Mini Beef and Cheese Empanadas	per empanada	280	19	11	240	18	0	2	1	7
Brazilian Cheese Bread (Pão de Queijo)	per roll	200	12	4.5	340	18	0	1	0	5
COOKIES & BARS										
Oatmeal–Chocolate Chip Cookies	per cookie	180	9	2.5	130	23	2	11	11	3
Chocolate Crinkle Cookies	per cookie	160	5	3	90	26	1	20	20	2
Chewy Peanut Butter Cookies	per cookie	190	9	2.5	160	23	1	16	15	4
Giant Chocolate Chip Cookie	serves 12	200	10	6	85	25	0	16	16	2
Jam Thumbprint Cookies	per cookie	80	3.5	2	45	11	0	6	3	1
Glazed Sugar Cookies	per cookie	90	5	3	50	8	0	1	1	1
Soft and Chewy Gingerbread People	per cookie	160	6	3.5	80	27	0	16	16	2
Mexican Wedding Cookies	per cookie	100	6	2.5	50	10	0	6	6	1
Coconut Macaroons	per cookie	110	8	7	65	9	1	7	3	1
Chewy Brownies	per brownie	190	9	3	80	26	1	19	19	2
Chewy Granola Bars with Cranberries and Walnuts	per bar	240	12	1	65	32	3	21	9	4
Key Lime Bars	per bar	150	6	4	80	20	0	17	3	3
Cheesecake Bars	per bar	200	12	8	140	17	0	14	13	3
CAKES & CUPCAKES										
Berry Snack Cake	serves 12	190	8	5	170	25	1	14	12	3
Easy Chocolate Snack Cake	serves 12	250	11	3	190	34	0	19	19	3
Tahini-Banana Snack Cake	serves 12	260	8	3	160	43	1	25	21	5

PER SERVING	CALORIES	FAT (G)	SATURATED FAT (G)	SODIUM (MG)	CARBOHYDRATES (G)	FIBER (G)	TOTAL SUGAR (G)	ADDED SUGAR (G)	PROTEIN (G)

CAKES & CUPCAKES

	PER SERVING	CALORIES	FAT (G)	SATURATED FAT (G)	SODIUM (MG)	CARBOHYDRATES (G)	FIBER (G)	TOTAL SUGAR (G)	ADDED SUGAR (G)	PROTEIN (G)
Gingerbread Snack Cake	serves 12	230	7	0.5	160	39	0	26	26	3
Pound Cake	serves 12	290	16	10	160	32	0	21	21	3
Yellow Sheet Cake with Chocolate Frosting	serves 18	460	28	16	190	50	0	35	26	5
Carrot Sheet Cake with Cream Cheese Frosting	serves 18	480	30	8	280	49	1	34	33	5
Yellow Cupcakes with Strawberry Frosting	per cupcake	400	23	14	310	42	0	29	27	5
Chocolate Cupcakes with Nutella Frosting	per cupcake	430	28	11	135	42	0	31	22	4
Confetti Layer Cake	serves 20	500	27	16	210	62	0	49	41	3
Confetti Frosting	per 2 tablespoons	150	9	6	15	15	0	15	12	0
Chocolate Frosting	per 2 tablespoons	170	13	8	10	14	0	11	5	1
Nutella Frosting	per 2 tablespoons	150	11	6	15	12	0	12	5	1
Cream Cheese Frosting	per 2 tablespoons	110	7	5	65	9	0	8	7	1
Strawberry Frosting	per 2 tablespoons	110	7	5	60	9	0	8	7	1
Cake Pops	per cake pop	140	8	4.5	60	17	0	13	6	2
Olive Oil Cake	serves 12	310	16	2.5	210	39	0	24	23	4
Mini Tea Cakes with Citrus Glaze	per mini cake	210	8	5	160	32	0	23	23	2
Individual Flourless Chocolate Cakes	per cake	370	26	15	135	36	2	32	32	4

FRUIT DESSERTS, PIES & TARTS

	PER SERVING	CALORIES	FAT (G)	SATURATED FAT (G)	SODIUM (MG)	CARBOHYDRATES (G)	FIBER (G)	TOTAL SUGAR (G)	ADDED SUGAR (G)	PROTEIN (G)
Apple Crisp	serves 8	230	8	4.5	40	41	3	25	13	2
Blueberry Cobbler	serves 8	300	9	5	350	54	3	32	20	4
S'mores Banana Boats	per banana	250	7	4.5	30	51	3	32	6	3
Free-Form Summer Fruit Tart	serves 8	310	17	11	150	36	2	15	9	4
Pumpkin Pie	serves 10	380	22	14	360	41	0	24	21	4
Lemon–Olive Oil Tart	serves 10	360	20	3.5	200	41	0	27	26	5
Cookies and Cream Ice Cream Pie	serves 10	300	15	7	160	39	0	27	0	3
Ruffled Milk Pie	serves 8	250	13	7	230	28	0	15	13	5
Raspberry Clafouti	serves 8	150	8	5	65	15	1	11	9	3

INDEX